THE
LOVE THEM
GOOD
BY
DOG
LEADING THEM
WAY

SEAN O'SHEA

The Good Dog Way: Love Them By Leading Them

Copyright © 2017 by Sean O'Shea

All Rights Reserved.

No part of this book may be reproduced in any form or by any means without permission in writing from the publisher, except for the inclusion of brief quotations in a review.

All information contained within this book is provided for recreational and educational purposes only, and should not be construed to be formal professional advice. By purchasing this book and using any of the advice set forth, there is no legal contract or formation of consultant-client relationship between Sean O'Shea, The Good Dog Training and Rehabilitation, The Good Dog Way, or any related person/entity and any individual person or entity.

ISBN: 978-0-692-85463-1

Cover by Mitransh Singh Parihar
mitransh_parihar@yahoo.com

Front cover & back cover photograph by Laura Morgan

Edited by Gidget Hall / Waypoint Copywriting
https://waypointcopywriting.com

Designed by Laura Morgan

Audiobook production by Micheal Ziants / Airlift Productions
mike@airliftproductions.com

People get dogs, and they end up struggling because they are giddy. That doesn't lead. That doesn't create a calm atmosphere. Give me gritty over giddy any day of the week. Gritty being the stuff shared that isn't "sexy." Isn't "fun." It's the "boring" stuff that gets the job done. The rules. Boundaries. 24 hr discipline. The giddy fun stuff is last on the list. Create giddy after the gritty.
-Chad Snow

Leadership is making the choice to do the right thing for your dog every time, even when it may be tough for either or both of you. It is prioritizing your dog's needs and quality of life above all your selfish desires. Leadership means continually learning to be a better leader every day for those that you are responsible for.
-Kalanit Azoulay

To me, leadership is taking someone under your wing of experience and guiding them to find their potential so they can be the best version of themselves…kinda like what you do for so many of us :)
-Lisa Healy

Leadership to me is being relevant to those around you in times of pressure and stress. Of serving as a point of reference behavior-wise for those you are fortunate enough to be entrusted to lead. Humans too:)
-Ashley Smentek

Leadership is built upon trust and a clear communication system. By providing positive feedback for correct choices, along with clear and fair expectations, steady guidance when clarity is needed, and being held accountable for incorrect choices, you create believable leadership.
-Alexis Hickson

To me, leadership is providing benevolent direction, protection, correction, and connection to the degree that it inspires those around you to follow.
-Kris Morin

The capacity to guide, to inspire, to course-correct and to decision-make.
-Denise McLeod

Leadership is being able to guide others on the way to success. To advocate for, and share valuable consequences for unwanted behavior. Recognizing and praising for good behavior. Being able to encourage and motivate others to accomplish their best in a fair fashion.
-Lise Lenny

Leadership is someone taking the helm so the crew can relax and do their jobs and or live their lives to their highest potential. It's seeing the sparkle in a diamond in the rough and lifting others up, by demanding their best so they can shine.
-Patti-Jean Trombley

Leadership: Setting rules and guidelines and motivating others to reach their full potential!
-Lauren Turner

Leadership is consistency in both reward and punishment. It's generosity in structure, guidance, security, and a labor of the utmost love. A dog that is properly led knows pride, safety, confidence, and affection. Along with a bond that strengthens and nurtures the heart and mind of both owner and pet.
-Michael Murphy

Leadership is knowing how to bring out the best qualities in others and encouraging them to do so.
-Jenn Gentile

Doing the hard work, not just what's fun, enables meaningful learning and connection in any relationship…both canine and human.
-Heather Ratcliff

Good leadership is making sure all those you are leading feel safe, secure, advocated for, and clearly know their jobs and what is expected of them.
-Michele Lilienthal

Leadership is teaching your dog yes and no out of love.
-Lita Scruton

Keeping your dogs safe and secure, and always feeling advocated for. Teaching clear boundaries for right and wrong.
-Destiny White

A well-behaved dog comes from a responsible owner. A human display of leadership is taking charge of, and responsibility for, your dog's actions. And guiding them to make the right choices!
-Nancy Labadie

A great leader is a great teacher. Great teachers know their students well, how to connect with them, when to teach, when to praise, when to correct, when to accept their limitations and when to challenge them to do more. Most importantly they know their potential and never accept their good-enough and always demand their best ever!
-Megan Dawn Romero

Leadership is making the choice to do the right thing for your dog every time, even when it may be tough for either or both of you. It is prioritizing your dog's needs and quality of life above all your selfish desires. Leadership means continually learning to be a better leader every day for those that you are responsible for.
-Natalie Lam

Recognize any of these names?

Probably not.

These aren't the vaunted names of highly-acclaimed dog trainers; mostly these are dog owners just like you. I asked them to share their personal thoughts on leadership so you could get some perspectives other than just mine. Often their words are even more powerful and succinct than my own.

I hope these quotes inspire you to explore the gifts of leadership.

Are you ready? Then let's go...

introduction
by Sean O'Shea

Some are just born with that special stuff. They have a confidence, a certainty, an air of authority. We all know when we're in their presence.

It can be inspiring and it can be daunting.

They know what to say, how to say it, when to act, when to stay put. They carry themselves in a certain fashion. They have that special thing. It's just that stuff.

This introduction isn't about one of "those" people.

This introduction is about me.

Yeah, I work with some of the most challenging dogs. Yeah, I teach owners how to find their confidence and self-trust. Yeah, some folks think I have some of that "special" stuff.

But you sure wouldn't have foreseen any of that if you could look back just a handful of years ago. Just a handful of years ago things were a little different.

I would have been called one of "those" owners by most trainers.

I would only use flat collars to walk my dogs because I was afraid I'd hurt them or their feelings. I would only use flexi-leashes because my dogs having fun and freedom was far more important than having any control or safety. I wouldn't use crates because heaven forbid my dogs should be locked in prison while I was away. Prong collars and E-collars...haha...you must be kidding.

I also leaned heavily on my dogs. I was a wreck emotionally. Work, money, family, relationships, self-worth...all of it was a mess. So my dogs became my safe place emotionally.

They were everything...and the only thing.

Everything was about making them happy. Because they were my only connection to happiness and love. So that was the only priority. And to be fair to me, I also didn't know anything about how to raise truly happy, balanced, well-behaved dogs.

I also didn't realize that all the stuff I thought I was doing to make my dogs "happy" was actually doing the exact opposite. They were stressed, anxious, overwhelmed, overly-stimulated and overly-aroused. They had no guidance, no structure, no rules, and no help to navigate this world. All the freedom, all the options, all the "yes's" and zero "no's" left them with zero clarity about what was right or wrong. What was expected, what was safe, and what wasn't.

I'd say they were alone, but that wouldn't be true. They had me encouraging and allowing all the worst stuff.

I was literally ruining my dogs by loving them without leading them. I just didn't know it.

My guys, Oakley (a 90-pound Pit mix) and Junior (a 67-pound Chow mix), who I adopted at 8 and 6 months respectively, were becoming a serious mess.

Oakley developed intense separation anxiety. He destroyed and consumed everything in my life. My apartment, my phone, my VHS tapes, my bed, my carpet, my door frames, my doors. When it got to the point that I couldn't leave him without me having a panic attack, I started taking him with me in my car. He ate that too. The steering wheel, the emergency brake, the seats.

Along with that, he was starting to show some intense reactivity on walks, and aggression towards other dogs.

Junior followed suit. Not in the destruction, but growling at me when I'd sit down too close to him on the couch, taking on a majorly bratty attitude, and plenty of reactivity on walks as well.

And forget about either of them listening to any commands.

When things were at their worst with the walks, they would explode, redirect on each other, lunge and pull at other dogs, and basically become menaces. Like many of my clients, I would hide behind cars, avoid other dogs like the plague, and become a stressed-out mess when we did encounter one.

I have vivid memories of taking my guys to the park for some adventures. And if getting pulled off your feet on wet grass and being dragged on your behind for a hundred yards or so towards other dogs in the distance sounds adventurous, then that's exactly what it was.

Or you could just call it humiliating. :)

Wanting my guys to have as much fun as possible (and feeling guilty for living in an apartment), we'd go to the hills for off-leash "hikes." These were essentially terror-filled events, where my guys, as soon as they were unleashed, would run as fast as they could...away from me. I'd spend the rest of the time trying to catch them.

If they got out the front door of my apartment while I was trying to walk out, forget it. You'd be chasing them for miles...and hoping they didn't attack any dogs on the way.

Terrible.

Things got worse and worse.

Eventually Oakley and Junior would attack any dog they could get to.

A couple of good friends, knowing how bad things were, recommended I check out a show called *The Dog Whisperer*. I chuckled when I heard the name. But my friends were smart folks, so I figured I'd at least check it out.

Like many people, I was swept away by watching dogs and owners transforming. The message: "It's at least as much you as it is your dog" struck a nerve. I'd never considered I might be part of the problem! Haha!

It's kind of amazing to think about now, but I really had no idea. *The Dog Whisperer* opened my eyes to *my* side of things. It showed me some actual approaches. And it really hit me that training could be about something far deeper than just teaching a dog to sit or roll over.

For me, this is where the change started. Regardless of what you think of the show or the man or the techniques, it was the turning point.

My entire mindset shifted.

I got to work, on me *and* my dogs. Big time. I immersed myself in personal development and self-help books. I devoured training videos and training books. I was hooked.

I changed my tools, moving to prong collars and 4-foot leashes. I worked on becoming aware of who and what I shared with my dogs. It was hard. My dogs had lots of memories of the old Sean, and they weren't going to let go of those easily. On top of that, I had developed acute anxiety from all the explosions and reactivity. Seeing dogs was incredibly challenging…both for my training mechanics and my mind.

To help flood myself and my dogs (a term I didn't even know about at the time), I would go to the local park where tons of people would walk their dogs on a giant rectangular tracks, all in one direction. Me and my guys? We'd walk *against* the onslaught. I figured if we only saw a dog sporadically, we'd all stay stuck. We needed a major overhaul.

So twice a day we went to this park and walked the gauntlet, in reverse. It wasn't pretty at first. I didn't know about using space, I didn't have very good (if any) technique, and I was terrified. I was also incredibly self-conscious about correcting my dogs in front of other people.

But we stayed the course. Literally. And slowly, ever so slowly, it started to shift…just a little. Then a little more. And then even more. Soon, we were kind of rock stars of the park. Some dogs could still be challenging, and I was learning about space and pressure…the hard way… but we were getting there.

Fast forward a year or so and I had a third dog, Belle. I found her on the 10 freeway standing in the fast lane. She was about a year old and was just about the most perfect dog you could ask for. The reward for the other two scoundrels! Haha.

The four of us would hustle all around Sherman Oaks. We were pretty striking. All my dogs were big, and almost exactly the same color. And they walked like angels. We covered miles and miles every morning and night. People would remark how well-behaved they were.

My confidence was starting to grow. I was morphing from the frightened, overwhelmed, uninformed, terrible dog owner, to someone with some of the best-behaved dogs in the neighborhood.

It was kind of amazing.

I was working on me and my dogs, and it was all starting to come together. One fateful day, a nice old lady pulled over and asked if I was a dog walker. I said "yes!"

She hired me, recommended me to all her friends, and soon I was a busy dog walker. And one who was developing a reputation for being able to handle really reactive, challenging dogs, and big packs. From there the move to training was a gradual, organic transition.

It wasn't long before the training business took over the walking business. Soon I was swamped with training clients. Mostly dogs that other trainers had struggled with or wouldn't work with.

And The Good Dog was born.

My hope of sharing this story with you guys isn't to celebrate my work or success. It's actually the opposite. I wanted to start this book by sharing my failures and struggles. To share with all of you that you don't have to be born with that "special" something.

You can be a mess.

You can do it all wrong.

You can be "that" owner.

I was. I've been there. I know what it's like.

And I'm here to remind you that if you want it to change, no matter how bad it's been, you can change it. If you're willing to do the hard work...on both of you.

-Sean O'Shea

Me, Oakley, and Junior circa 2003.

part ONE
the gap

the 10/10 principle:

What's the number one question we get from owners?

"When can we pet him?"

When can we love on him? When can he be on the couch? When can he have total freedom?

Okay, that's several questions, but you get the idea, right?

When people get dogs, they don't get them thinking they'll have to restrict their affection. They don't think couch privilege might not be on the menu. They don't think they'll have to restrict their dog's ability to roam the house. But, if things have gone sideways with their dog's behavior and their relationship with their dog, changing or adjusting these things might just be what's needed to help sort that behavior and relationship stuff out.

What many owners don't understand is that these seemingly benign privileges and interactions can create strong feelings and perceptions in our dogs, feelings and perceptions about *us*, their owners. Feelings of permissiveness, softness, neediness, feeling like we might just be ripe for the taking advantage of. With certain dogs, these interactions and privileges we share can unintentionally convey that listening, respecting, and prioritizing us isn't something they need to worry about. And this can cause lots of problems.

You may see horrible behavior on walks, territorial stuff around the house or yard, possessiveness, guarding, neurotic barking, fighting amongst household dogs, fear and nervousness, or even human aggression.

But here's the thing: these privileges and interactions, on their own, aren't the sole cause of the problems. Actually, they can be almost totally benign.

So then what's the problem?

The problems arise when these privileges and interactions occur in the absence of their counterbalance: the training, leadership, rules, authority, and accountability. It's when the conversation is completely lopsided that things get funky.

Owners don't realize they're having a one-sided, dysfunctional conversation with their dogs that's leading things astray. They don't realize they're giving all the privileges, freedom, and love, without asking for anything in return. When things are given excessively, freely, with no boundaries, and with no demands for corresponding good behavior, things can get ugly, fast.

Respect can go out the window, and dogs can get stressed, anxious, nervous, opportunistic, and freaked out!

So trainers, looking to shore things up, even things out, and re-balance the human-to-dog conversation, ask owners to remove or reduce certain privileges and interactions. The goal is to shift the way your dog feels about you and your household back to a more healthy space, and thus, get your dog himself to shift back to a more healthy space. And usually, when things are just beginning, when you're just starting to work on resetting your dog and your relationship, we want to create as much leverage as possible; to create the strongest perceptions we can. So we go hard on the changes. Perhaps zero affection. Perhaps zero roaming. Perhaps zero furniture access. But that's only half of the equation. It's not just about what we remove, it's also about what we add that really makes things click...

The discipline, the rules, the accountability. The elements that make room for all the fun stuff. The elements that keep the other side of your conversation in balance.

But what about those inevitable questions we started out with? When can owners loosen up? When can they have more of the fun stuff?

Honestly, it depends on the dog, and it depends on you. It depends on how bad things have been, how out of balance you both are, and perhaps most importantly, what you're capable of sharing in regards to the other side of the conversation. The leadership conversation.

And this is where our 10/10 Principle comes in.

On our scale, if you're a 2 in the leadership/rules department, you better be a 2 in the affection/freedom department. If you're a 6 in the leadership/rules department, then you can be a 6 in the affection/freedom department. See how it works? It's just about balancing the conversation, so your dog stays … **balanced.** Your job is to make sure your numbers line up as best you can.

If you're an 8 in affection and freedom, and a 2 in discipline, you're gonna have issues!

The truth is, most owners struggle with the discipline side of things. They struggle with the rules, the enforcement, the structure; so keeping an eye on the corresponding freedoms and affection is essential. But the great thing is, if you want more of the fun stuff, you simply need to up your other game. It's not a static thing. Change the leadership number, and you'll eventually get to change the freedom number. How much, and to what degree depends on you and your dog as individuals. But there's always room for growth.

If you'll use the 10/10 scale - honestly! - it can help you navigate the tough questions above, and help guide you towards a more healthy, rewarding, and ultimately fun relationship.

what's up for GRABS?

What's up for grabs? The house? The yard? The other dog? The food? The bone? That spot on the floor? The couch?

You?

If you don't own your world, there's a good chance your dog will. Territorial issues, dog fights, possessive issues, hyper-protective issues. Not to mention fear, stress, and anxiety problems.

Leadership, in the form of owning, and then sharing your world, is the antidote for so many serious behavior issues. 🐾

what are you SAYING?

Everything you do, say, ask for, allow, prevent, address, **or not**, is saying something about you and your expectations for your dog and his or her relationship with you.

Your actions are always talking, and your dog is always listening. 🐾

Dogs do what they're allowed to do. **It's that simple.**

If they bark, it's because you allow it.
If they jump, it's because you allow it.
If they run away, it's because you allow it.
If they guard, it's because you allow it.
If they fight, it's because you allow it.
If they're jealous, it's because you allow it.
If they're nasty with other dogs, it's because you allow it.
If they're possessive, it's because you allow it.
If they're crazy on walks, it's because you allow it.
If they bark, snap, or growl at people, it's because you allow it.

This doesn't mean you've wanted to allow these things. This doesn't mean you've intentionally encouraged them. You probably haven't known how to address or stop them, and that's okay, but understanding the simplicity of how these issues start, continue, and grow is essential to changing them. Once you get that allowing is a necessary component of all this stuff, you can go after it.

Because the only thing that can impact and alter your dog's behavior issues is you. Your job is to own that, and then figure out how to change what you don't want.

If you don't want it, don't allow it. Simple and hard all at the same time. :)

BAR or THERAPIST?

They both offer help.

The first offers immediate relief from pain and discomfort. It creates the illusion of healing, aids in avoiding the painful things we need to work on and work through, and eventually causes dependency. Repeated long enough, it not only prevents you from making any progress on your true issues, but it guarantees those issues will spiral to even darker and more painful depths.

The second usually doesn't provide instant results. It's hard, messy, uncomfortable, often downright painful, but eventually, with effort and consistency, provides real help, insight, and true healing.

The challenge here is that one is instant and easy, and the other delayed and hard.

And like us, our dogs are masters at choosing the easiest and most immediate route of relief from anything they're uncomfortable with.

If they're nervous/unsure/fearful of men, kids, cars, manhole covers, dogs, whatever, they'll either avoid them, react to them, or try to attack them, all in an effort to find immediate relief. Unfortunately that relief doesn't change how they actually feel about the trigger, it just temporarily sidesteps it. So the issue with the trigger festers and deepens, and reactions get worse.

As our dog's owners and stewards, we have the job of seeing the bigger picture. It's up to us to see the problems our dogs are dealing with and make smart choices about how to help, even if those choices require some discomfort and taking our dogs out of their comfort zones.

We have the choice of either becoming the bar or the therapist.

Do we hug, coddle, and try to love them through their fears, or do we ask them to stand up to them? Do we create stories and excuses for their behavior, or do we own up to reality? Do we become partners and enablers in their avoidance, or do we decide to tackle the issues? Do we lock them away to avoid their triggers, or do we find a way to help them better cope and deal?

The truth is, we get to choose which path we take; easy or hard, hiding or breaking through. Our dogs need us to choose for them. 🐾

fixing dogs

There's a lot of talk in training circles and with owners about "fixing" dogs...

And the concept is a dangerous one. It puts unrealistic pressure and expectations on trainers, owners, and dogs. Everyone has been led to believe that a total fix is totally possible, and anything less than a total fix is a gap in training or ownership.

But to imagine that a dog, this incredibly complex emotional being, with whatever genetic material and baggage it comes with, whatever prior experience baggage it comes with, and whatever personality or individuality it comes with, to be something that can be transformed into something completely different than what it is and what it contains, is just kind of silly.

Imagining dogs can be "fixed" is like imagining that you, with all of your past experiences, traumas, challenges, personality, attitudes, and genetics, could be perfect, or issue-free. You can do as much therapy, self-help, and personal work as possible, and you can make enormous strides, and transformations, but you will still be you. You will still have your quirks. You will still have your tendencies. You can become the very best you, but it will still be you.

And you won't be perfect or fixed.

And that's the truth with dogs as well. It's not a negative or a letdown, it's simply a reset about reality and having appropriate, healthy expectations.

Can you make amazing, wild, mind-blowing transformations in problem dogs? Absolutely! I see it every day. But, these dogs aren't fixed, nor have they had their individuality — genetics, experience, personality — removed and replaced! No, they've simply been made a better version of themselves. And that should be the goal (and expectation) for both the dog owner and the dog trainer—to make the dog the best version of himself that is possible. Some dogs will be able to make more progress than others. Some will have more limitations than others. And that's just like it is with us. We're all individuals, and that's both the beauty and the challenge.

Because none of us get fixed, but we all can improve.

movement is EASY; stillness is HARD.

Most folks focus way too much on the movement in training and not nearly enough on the staying put!

And for most dogs, that suits them just fine. Why? Because movement is easy for dogs. It's one of their easiest and most readily used ways of coping with stress or excess nervous energy. But it doesn't effectively deal with either, it just masks the problem (Think of you using email, alcohol, or video games to distract yourself from your own "stuff").

Dogs that are in constant motion, pacing, running fences, following owners, barking, or chasing stuff, are not relaxed dogs. They're dogs on edge. They're dogs that are worked up and uncomfortable. And worked up, uncomfortable dogs make all kinds of bad choices.

Everyone seems to think the more motion and action the better it is for the dog. But that's often not the case. Teaching dogs how to slow down, chill-out, and become relaxed observers of their worlds, rather than constantly on-edge reactors to it is where much of the mental transformation comes from. This is where calm, relaxed, comfortable, **well-behaved** dogs come from.

Teaching dogs to override their impulse to be in constant motion and activity is a simple, but profoundly effective training approach. We call it duration work or doggy meditation. 45, 60, 90 minute (or more!) place and/or down commands are easy ways to create this.

Often it's the missing piece of the training puzzle.

I talk a lot about **leadership**, and very little about **companionship** in regards to dog training, or just living with your dog. Here's why:

Hanging out, doing what feels good, being "buddies," sharing affection, just enjoying each other (companionship) are all easy. That's the stuff we see ALL of our clients doing, without coaching or prompting. It's the stuff that folks enjoy, easily gravitate to, and share with their dogs in abundance. It's also the stuff that, in the absence of leadership, unhinges many relationships.

Leadership, on the other hand, is the hard stuff.

It's the stuff that isn't as fun; the stuff that demands you do the uncomfortable or not-easy, in order to create a balanced dog and relationship. It's where you prioritize your dog's needs over your own. Where you sometimes do what isn't as fun or enjoyable in order to **create balance**.

companionship
vs.
LEADERSHIP

In all my days as a trainer, working with over a thousand dogs, I can count on one hand (actually make that two fingers) how many times I've had to coach an owner to be more loving, affectionate, easy-going, and permissive. Twice! LOL. But I have constantly had to coach folks how to shift gears and adjust to being firmer, sharing more rules, more accountability, and less affection and freedom.

Let's connect this with actual parenting. It's easy to be your kid's buddy — to do all the fun stuff — and much harder to be your kid's parent. The parent is the one who isn't always popular, and who has to be the heavy when necessary. The one who is actually in charge, who creates rules and boundaries and enforces them, because they make for a happier child (and adult) in the long run.

So I'm always reminding folks about leadership, the hard stuff, because companionship, the easy stuff, is, well...**easy.**

LEADERSHIP=COMFORT

When we know what's expected of us...
When we know what the rules are...
When we know that consequences are real...
When we know someone has been there before...
When we know things are predictable...
When we know if we get off track we'll be guided back...
When we know there aren't a million options...
When we know we're protected...
When we know we're safe...

We feel comfort.

We crave it, and so do our dogs.

Intention matters

It's not just about tools, and it's not just about training strategies and methods.

The real fuel for our success, in any endeavor, but especially so with our dogs, starts with our **intention**, our **belief**, and our **mental commitment to the outcome we desire**. The intention you bring to the moment affects every part of your being, and it either fuels your believability or reveals your uncertainty. Dogs are masters at reading intention, certainty, and believability. So remember, before you attempt to tackle that big dog issue or training exercise, *get your mindset right*.

Decide what you will accomplish, see yourself kicking butt, visualize how it will look when done, and commit 100% to creating your outcome. Your results might just surprise you.

You got this.

One of the essential secrets to being successful with your dog is for your dog to believe that you've got him.

That you're able to manage and control yourself when the chips are down, AND you're able to do the same for him by giving the direction and guidance he needs to feel safe and comfortable. Just *wanting* your dog to be well-behaved and safe isn't enough. You've got to *create* this reality, and you create this by proving to him that **the rules are real, that consequences are real, that your guidance is real, and that he can trust you to be there** — not just for the easy, fun stuff, but also for the harder, more challenging and sometimes less fun stuff.

By going out and proving to your dog every day that you've got him and that you've got this, you'll see remarkable changes in his choices, behavior, and overall comfort level. And it also feels pretty good for you!

Lead more, follow less

At some point, we lost our way. We shifted. We went from being the ones who laid down the rules, enforced the rules, and kept our dogs in a healthy, polite space, to becoming enabling, spoiling, guilt-ridden followers.

I know that sounds harsh, but it's unfortunately true. Much of what constitutes good training is simply about returning that balance of leadership to the equation. It's so simple that it's easy to overlook or dismiss. But it's THE essential component to a well-behaved, balanced dog.

would you FOLLOW YOU?

One of the most important questions we can ask ourselves when working with dogs is: **Are we someone worth following?**

Are you consistent and dependable? Do you do what you say? Do you react or respond? Are you overly stressed or anxious? Do you have temper issues? Are you plagued by insecurity? Do you take responsibility or blame others? Are you able to clearly set boundaries and communicate what's okay and what's not okay? Do you own your space and beliefs? Are you as firm as you are loving? Are you consumed by loneliness and disconnection? Are you someone you're proud of?

As valuable as training is for our dogs, making sure we're becoming the very best versions of ourselves — doing our own work — is even more important.

So before we ask our dogs to follow us, first we have to ask ourselves:
Would you follow you? 🐾

power of INFLUENCE

We all become what we surround ourselves with daily.

That's why all success coaches remind us to be acutely aware of who and what we spend our time with — because we become what we expose ourselves to daily.

And of course, it's the same with our dogs.

Whatever we surround them with daily they're going to absorb and pick up.

Are we stressed? Impatient? Anxious? Fearful? Impulsive? Manic? Always excited? Unsure of ourselves? Angry? Judgmental? Worried constantly? Always in a rush, or needy?

All these ways of being will have an impact on the humans in your life AND the dogs in your life. But the humans usually have the ability to take a break, take a breather, go for a drive, leave the house, leave the situation, or simply set up boundaries. Dogs are stuck.

So what we tend to see is our dogs slowly absorbing and taking on the qualities we share with them daily.

Now, this doesn't mean that our dogs will take on carbon copy behaviors of ours. No, they may take on totally different qualities, but they're most definitely affected by what you share.

The always-excited, manic owner may create an excited, manic dog. Or he might create a nervous, insecure, freaked out dog. It all depends on the dog's personal makeup.

Looking for exact, mirror behavior is likely to confuse you, because you may see the opposite. But that doesn't mean it's not still the influence in action.

The best suggestion is to become aware of your own behavior. Become sensitive to who you are and what you share with the world, with both dogs and people. Watch your dog to see if he has become less comfortable, less well-behaved, more neurotic, more troubled. Perhaps more like you, perhaps less. Just know that we can't live with each other day in and day out and NOT have an impact and influence on each other. We're ALWAYS impacting and influencing. The question is, is it positive or negative? Or a little of both?

P.S. Dogs also come with their own "stuff." So your behavior likely isn't the sole cause of whatever issues your dog is sharing. Your job is to be aware of where and when your stuff is becoming your dog's stuff.

Dogs are smart.

They know what works and what doesn't.

Have you ever seen a dog try to dig a hole in cement? I don't mean scratch at it momentarily; I mean a concerted, committed, ongoing effort to create a hole in the cement.

I know I haven't.

So why? It's a perfectly good surface to scratch or dig on.

Because **cement doesn't give**. At all. And once dogs realize this, they abandon the dig. It's no fun; it's not getting them anywhere, it's a dead end.
What wise and informed insights can we glean from this deep observation?

"CEMENT DOESN'T GIVE."

Simple.

Whatever "gives" will receive continued effort and focus, whatever doesn't, won't.

This goes for straightforward stuff like crates (if you've got a crate breaker, getting a special crate with zero give, or reinforcing the one you have is a necessity), all the way to the more nuanced stuff like consistency with rules. If you allow rules to be occasionally flexed, expect them to be flexed often.

Dogs are smart. They're looking for stuff that "gives" in order for them to get more of what they want, whatever that want might be. Your job is to be aware of this, and make sure that the stuff you're trying to help your dog with, or rules that are important to you, don't give.

REAL talk

If you've got a tough, pushy, strong willed, challenging dog, it's time for the shift.

The shift from dog lover to dog leader, from playmate to parent, **from kissing ass to kicking ass.** 🐾

resistance IS NOT futile

The bratty dog who successfully resists offers more brattiness in the future. The nervous dog who successfully resists offers more nervousness in the future. The aggressive dog who successfully resists offers more aggression in the future. And the fearful dog who successfully resists offers more fear in the future.

This successful resistance reinforces that these choices, regardless of how unhealthy, work.

They get the dog what it wants in that moment...as quickly as possible. And that success leads to more and more of whatever the dog might be doing.

The patterns become deeper, the habits stronger, and eventually, what started out as momentary choices and behaviors, start to become the dog's personality. Their way of being.

But if we block these choices, and prevent unhealthy resistance, we open the door to leading our dogs towards a more happy and healthy life. 🐾

If you want to build muscle, you have sweat it out at the gym.

If you want to gain knowledge, you have to do the hard work of studying and focusing.

If you want to succeed at your job or craft, you have put in massive hours and push yourself past your comfort zone.

If you want to resolve emotional pain, you have to be willing to wade into the dark waters of therapy.

All this stuff is hard, challenging, and uncomfortable.

what's HARD is GOOD

But it's precisely what allows us to come out better on the other side.

It's the same with your dog. If you want her to be her best, you can't just do the easy stuff. You have to look for the weak spots and problem areas.

Are there fears? **Go after them.**
Are there distractions that overwhelm? **Go after them.**
Are there certain behaviors that just seem like they won't stop? **Go after them.**

The weak spots should always be your focus points. The problem areas point you in the direction that needs attention.

It's the hard stuff that leads the way to the good stuff.

"The consequence that's valuable is the one your dog decides is valuable,

not you."

5 DOLLAR SPEEDING TICKET

How much impact would a 5 dollar speeding ticket have on you? Probably not much. Would it change your love of speed? The need to get across town just a shade faster because you're late? Your impatient nature? Nah. 5 bucks is just a nice latte.

If the consequence for speeding is so tiny, speeding looks awfully good...whatever the reason.

Now let's have some fun. Imagine the standard speeding ticket was **5,000 bucks**...no matter what the reason, or how little you happened to be creeping over the limit. How might that affect your driving habits? I'd guess, a whole lot.

Even if you REALLY liked the adrenaline rush of a little heavy footing. Even if you were late for a REALLY important appointment. Even if you were REALLY the impatient type.

I'd bet you'd make some very different decisions...

"When consequences become significant, behavior changes..."

"for all of us."

So, same reasons and attractions, but totally different reactions.

What changed? Just the monetary consequence, and the awareness of what that consequence might mean to you. **$5k is a lot of dough.**

In dog-land I see the five dollar speeding ticket issued a bunch. And guess what goes along with that? Yep, not much.

Owners might try to override chasing a squirrel with a stern yell, jumping by ignoring, pulling by standing still, or counter surfing by grabbing the dog's collar and having a firm conversation about the dangers involved with scarfing unauthorized goodies, etc.

They're unaware that they're underwhelming their dog. The rewards simply outweigh the consequences. And when that's the case, the rewards that are most valuable (according to your dog, not you), **get picked every time.**

Doing the wrong thing is supposed to be uncomfortable. The whole point of a speeding ticket is the discomfort. The discomfort (or awareness of its possibility) is what changes our behavior.

And it's the same for our dogs.

Consequences, both positive and negative, drive all our behavior. If they're meaningless, you can count on whatever behavior you're trying to stop...to continue. 🐾

BLURRED LINES

So how come things have gotten so much more dicey with our dogs?

How come there seems to be far more ill-behaved dogs than the "good old days?"

How come there's so much aggression, resource guarding, possessiveness, separation anxiety, reactivity, and so on?

Am I just out of touch and remembering romantically those past days when dogs seemed to be dogs and humans seemed to be humans – and both seemed to be the better for it?

I'm not so sure. I'm 48. I was born in the late 60's. I remember very clearly the way our dogs lived with us (and the way most of my friend's dogs did as well). Our dogs were far from perfect, but I don't remember hearing much about many of the above issues. There was "dog world" and "human world."

But, boy, things have changed.

These days, most dogs live inside. They share our personal and intimate space freely. But that's not all that's changed. Along with the physical access, they've also moved inside our hearts and minds in a way that typically didn't exist previously. Not that previous generations didn't love their dogs, I'm sure they did, but the role our dogs play in our emotional lives today seems much different than that of the past. This has created a lot of negative fallout for our dogs, and for us who share our lives with them.

I love having my dogs inside. I'd hate to live with my crew outside. My guys are allowed on furniture, sleep on my bed, and roam the house pretty much as they please. We share the space. My guys are also very important to me emotionally. They're still dogs, but they hold a special place in my heart, and I think that's pretty clear to them.

So this begs the question: with this new dynamic of near total integration and sharing, how the heck do you keep your dogs balanced, respectful, polite, and well-behaved in the face of all these mixed messages?

My feeling is this: Once we took our dogs inside, once we made them our daily physical and emotional companions, it changed what was required of us. Our parents (or maybe *you* if you're of that older generation) could probably get away with not doing as much training. They likely didn't need to create a ton of structure, hone their leadership skills, or use the same tools and strategies to keep their dogs balanced. Their dogs were dogs. But for us, with these blurred lines, we've got a different reality.

Because we've shifted our dogs' perceptions of us, because we've integrated them so deeply into our lives, because we've leaned so hard on them emotionally – many becoming surrogate children, spouses, or friends – we've got a whole different reality. A reality where we have to work a heck of a lot harder to keep them balanced.

Once we brought them into our world in this more intimate fashion, things changed. Our jobs as dog owners got harder, more complex. Our responsibilities, if we are to have healthy, balanced dogs, got heavier and more challenging.

The upshot is we've fundamentally changed how we live and interact with our dogs. There's no getting around it, and I don't think it's changing any time soon. Our dogs have become central players in our lives; family members we cherish and adore. And that's not necessarily a bad thing … IF we're prepared to do the hard work that comes with that.

With this new way of living comes greater challenges– the possibility of neurotic behavior, feelings of entitlement, boundary pushing, disrespect and lots more. For me, the answer was to make sure that as deep as I loved, and as much freedom I granted, that I shared equally firm, unquestionable discipline. While my guys know I love them deeply, they also know that any monkey business is met with firm, immediate, and valuable consequences. That balance of love and leadership is what allows me to have the best of both worlds.

It's work my folks and their friends likely never had to do, at least not at this level. For the most part, they chose to have their dogs be dogs, and that meant an easier human/dog lifestyle path in many ways. But that might also have meant the absence of intimate dog companionship, and perhaps lonely outdoor lives for many dogs. So there are trade-offs in both. But for those of us choosing to live in the more integrated fashion, remember that freedom, connection and enjoyment comes at a cost–*if* we want to have happy, healthy dogs we can enjoy.

And that cost is more awareness, more responsibility, more effort, and the willingness to share as much discipline as we share love. 🐾

What happens when your doctor tells you your cholesterol is dangerously high? What happens when your spouse threatens to leave because of your behavior? What happens when your accountant tells you you've spent far more than you've earned?

you,

Well, if any of the above matter to you, several things should happen. One, it should create some fear (what happens if I don't change this?). Two, it should create some serious contemplation (how can I avoid this in the future?). Three, it should create some new decisions (I'll do this new thing instead and bypass the bad stuff.).

All of the above serve a valuable purpose. They're reminders about impending consequences... *if the behavior doesn't change.* Gifts that help get you back on the right path.

And it's the same for your dogs. Except *you're* the one issuing the warnings. You're the one helping your dog steer through this crazy world as safely and comfortably as possible.

your dog,

The context will be different. Your dog won't be getting into the same pickles as you, but the outcomes can be just as dire, if not worse.

Dogs get hit by cars, returned to shelters for jumping/barking/destruction, die from obstructions, and are often just major stressors for their owners. It's your job to make sure they stay safe, fit into human life, and have the simple clarity of what's right and wrong.

and CONSEQUENCES

But in our current dog owning/training culture, consequences (also known as information or feedback) have become something only the mean or uninformed share with their dog. If utilized, these nasty things will crush your dog's spirit and damage your relationship.

So rather than that, it's recommended that you ignore the bad and reward the good.

But what if life treated you the same way? What if your doctor ignored your cholesterol count but said, "Nice work, you lost a pound"? What if your spouse ignored your inability to manage your anger issues, but said, "You were lovely tonight" when you didn't explode for a change? What if your accountant ignored your spending issues but said, "Nice work on only spending 5k over your budget" rather than the usual 10k?

What would happen is, you'd be robbed of essential information and feedback. Stuff you desperately need to better navigate life. Consequences are there to help you understand something needs to change. That something is putting you in danger. That something isn't in your best interests. They're not mean or nasty, they're just reality. They're just life. And without them, you're basically flying blind.

And so, in an interest to be kinder to our dogs, to ensure they don't experience undue stress or unhappiness...you know, that *learning stuff*...we shelter them from clarity. We shield them from the truth. We give them just a teeny piece of the life puzzle and ask them to figure out the rest. We make their lives infinitely harder, more stressful, and more dangerous.

How strange that this new, enlightened approach to kindness and love, actually ends up being the harshest treatment of all.

order in the COURT!

What keeps the peace? What prevents bad choices? What causes all of us to do our best work, play by the rules, and honor the rules of society?

Consequences.

The understanding that valuable, significant, and unsavory consequences will be delivered for making unsavory and unacceptable choices.

It's the same for our dogs as it for us.

We all want to make it more complicated, but behavior is always controlled by consequences. Once the rules, the structure, and the framework of expectations are fairly taught and shared, it's then up to consequences to ensure they're adhered to.

Miss this aspect, and you'll find yourself and/or your dog in trouble.

Keep it simple, keep it honest, keep it effective.

I've had my Tibetan Mastiff since he was a puppy at 12 weeks old.

I have never had this breed before but read up quite a bit on it, knowing after what I had read, I knew he had to go to training immediately. We bonded immediately, and I got to work socializing him with everybody and every thing.

It didn't work.

I put him into what I thought was the best training at the time for 2 weeks, mainly for his aggression at such a young age, but didn't really work out. He learned the basics, come, sit, how to walk on a lead, but the aggression was still there.

Gus was unpredictable. Friendly one minute, then he would turn only on certain people. Not all the time, not all people. For no reason, he would just go after somebody.

After 3 more years and a few incidents with his aggression, now a full grown adult 130 lb. dog, I searched for another trainer. I spoke with the owner and told him about my situation, and he assured me he could help. I scheduled another board and train at the facility 6 months in advance and had several conversations with the owner before our arrival date.

Long story short, the owner called me after just 2 hrs to come pick up my dog. They couldn't even get him out of the crate, not due to his aggression, but his separation anxiety. They told me he may have heart attack it was so bad. I did stay and did daily training for 2 weeks, but did not solve his aggression issues.

I was about to give up, and at one time thought about putting my beautiful boy down, when I came across a video on Facebook. It was the Good Dog Training video with Sean and his staff. I immediately called and spoke with Laura, and once again I was assured they could help.

What did I have to lose, except for my dog?

I took the chance and scheduled a board and train. They discussed the method of training, E-collar, and I was immediately on board with it.

After the initial meet and greet, I had high hopes for my dog Gus. I myself had a lot of homework to do. This was our last chance, and I prayed this training would help.

Gus is very stubborn, very strong-willed, and independent, and it took some time to get through to him, but eventually, Sean and his wonderful staff did. He responds to me, obeys me, and, although his aggression is still there, they taught me how to deal with it in a more manageable way.

It is my job to protect him as he protects me, meaning not to put him in unsafe situations. He is a one person dog; I don't need people to accept him or love on

him. He doesn't need playmates, and he is now controlled with an E-collar. We are able to walk together, he runs free on our ranch and comes when he's called. He places when he is supposed to, and it seems that he is a much happier dog, trying to please me with our daily exercises. There is structure in our lives now.

Sean and his staff at The Good Dog Training literally saved our lives, both Gus's and mine. He is part of the family and it would have been devastating if I had to put him down.

Just a note, I have had many big dogs in the past; a wolf-hybrid for 14 years, many German Shepherds, and even a pitbull. This breed, however, is more difficult than any of those breeds. Very headstrong, over-protective, unpredictable, and aloof.

Thank you TGD. I am forever grateful for the training for both him and me and for not giving up on us.

Keep up the amazing work and saving lives, one dog at a time.

the Lord of the Flies principle

If you have a multi-dog household and are experiencing tension, squabbles, or all-out fights, the reason is almost always a lack of leadership, structure, and rules. It's this gap that creates the opportunity for chaos.

When dogs don't have a strong pack structure in their house – meaning if they're not 100% sure who's in charge, what's allowed and not allowed, and that someone will effectively enforce the rules – they can quickly become **stressed, anxious, pushy, bratty, possessive, worried, fearful...and opportunistic.**

As you can imagine, dogs co-habitating in this fashion are going to be ripe for trouble and fighting. If you've ever read The Lord Of The Flies (I know this is going back a ways!), you've got a great example of the psychological and behavioral breakdown that occurs when structure, rules, and authority are absent. Just replace all the kids in the story with your dogs. :)

When structure, rules, and authority are absent, *stress, anxiety, and fear start to manifest.*

Why?

Because of survival instincts. Social creatures understand that the absence of structure, rules, and authority mean danger, risk, and fear...and that puts everyone on edge. Once that gap is created, safety becomes questionable. Behavior erratic. Anything can happen. Stress soars. And when that's the pervasive feeling, everyone starts to look out for their best interests, regardless of how it affects others.

Personality traits that might have remained managed or suppressed, in the presence of authority, begin to surface when that authority pressure is removed. Instead of dogs doing their best, we see them offering their worst.

Remember the end of the story, when the boys were finally rescued? They immediately reverted back to their normal, courteous, polite, thoughtful, and civilized selves. Why? Because they had to–and also because **they wanted to.** 🐾

theGIFT

Instead of simply being upset, annoyed, frazzled, or frustrated with your dog's behavior, ask yourself if there's a gift for yourself in the problem.

Are your dog's issues offering you an opportunity to challenge yourself, to grow, to become more? More confident, more emotionally balanced, less anxious, less in a hurry, more apt to look for answers than anger?

Are your dog's issues exposing issues for yourself that need work?

It's a very rare appointment in which the dog I'm working with isn't reacting to some degree to the human's issues and/or wouldn't benefit from the human growing, challenging, progressing, developing themselves into more fully balanced, healthy versions of themselves.

If you only look for the problem your dog is offering, that is all you'll find. But if you'll take a deeper, more honest, and vulnerable look, you'll find the gift he is offering as well.

"When it comes to our dogs, we always have a choice. The choice to see problems or to see opportunities."

the amazing dog (you don't have)

You might just have an amazing dog.

You might just have a really well-behaved dog.

You might just have a dog that would get complimented by strangers (no way!!). You might just have a dog you'd be super proud of that you could take anywhere.

You might just have this dog, sitting right under your nose…misbehaving, acting crazy, getting into trouble all over the place…being a wreck.

The truth is, until you actually train your dog, demand his best, set high expectations, clearly guide him regarding what's right and wrong, **and** enforce the rules when broken, you'll never know the dog you actually have.

We've had zillions of "crazy," "out of control," "annoying," "aggressive," "disrespectful" dogs come through our doors in one state, and leave out the same door in an entirely different state. And with an entirely different set of descriptive words.

Words like "amazing," "a totally different dog," "a pleasure to be around," "he's so smart," "he actually listens," "he's so calm" etc.

How upset would you be to find out you've had a Ferrari in your garage all these years, and no one told you?

While your dog might not ever be "perfect," I know from experience that most owners are astonished at what their dog — that same dog that has been driving them nuts and derailing their life - is actually capable of!

Yep, you might just (and probably do!) have an amazing dog under all that chaos and craziness, but you'll never know until you do the work. Amazingness, in any form, comes with a price tag. And it's no different with your dog. Don't assume crazy is your dog's only gear — it's likely the only gear you've taught him.

Often the difference between teasing out the awesome in your dog, or continuing to struggle, is simply based on knowledge and awareness. Using the wrong tools or approach could stymie even a ton of effort. If you've been working hard, but not seeing the desired results, it might be time to reevaluate both.

Something that I think is easy to lose sight of is the unrealistic pursuit of perfection.

It's so easy to see someone's dog doing amazing in a context that yours struggles in and to feel defeated. It's so easy to see training videos and marketing of dogs

imperfect DOGS

doing fantastic, amazing things and feel deflated. And it's so easy to feel hyper self-aware of all of you and your dog's shortcomings in the face of people who don't understand your battle and all the hard work you've put in.

It's so easy to see everyone else's perfect dog, especially if yours has some more pronounced issues going down, but the truth is, there are no perfect dogs. Every dog, including mine, has their "stuff." Now this "stuff" might be mild or it might be serious, but they all have it.

Now this doesn't mean we simply accept them where they're at and don't work our butts off to improve them — that would be doing them and us a huge disservice. But it does mean that it's super important for all of us to hold onto some perspective.

Yeah, our dogs may have some issues, but the thing is, us humans always see our world much clearer and more pronounced than we do the world of others. We don't see the owner with the perfect walking dog who never barks being a wreck at the vet. We don't see the perfectly relaxed family dog who doesn't jump or bark when you come into their house go bananas on the walk at the little white fluff ball. We're not privy to everyone else's moments, so we judge based on what we see, and what we see is so limited. We only see their good and our bad, and we judge our dogs and ourselves accordingly. But if you could see everyone else's dogs in their least best moments — even rockstar dogs that you'd think would be problem-free—you'd feel a whole lot better about you and yours. Promise.

Like us, every dog is both flawed and special. They each have their strengths and weaknesses. Our job is to do our best to enhance those strengths and diminish those weaknesses. BUT, the magic is in keeping the proper perspective. Remembering that we're all fighting battles and struggles and that just because you don't always see them, doesn't mean they aren't happening. And that perhaps sharing a little empathy with you and your dog (or with others if you're the judgy one!) as you work through the process, is the important shift. The shift that ensures you enjoy this journey of improvement, and who's on it with you, rather than simply focusing on a perfect destination that doesn't actually exist.

FAULTY

There are dogs out there, that no matter how much training, and how good the training, no matter which tools, and no matter how much resolve you bring, will still struggle.

As a business that focuses primarily on serious behavior modification, we probably see more of this than most. Because we're often the 2nd, 3rd, or 4th trainer an owner and dog sees, and because we've positioned ourselves as a place for the most serious issues, we're in somewhat of a unique position.

We see the dogs that have struggled with all types of training and tools. We see the owners that are 100% committed, but still getting nowhere.

Of course, these are the exceptions. The one-percenters. Most dogs thrive when the right training, tools, and owner mindset meet. Almost all of them. But there are the exceptions. There are the dogs that just aren't put together right mentally. Dogs that didn't get crucial early experiences. Dogs who process, feel, and react far different than your normal dog.

Luckily, I can count these guys on two hands. Out of over a thousand dogs trained, there are probably only around ten that qualify. But they're out there, nonetheless.

dogs

These guys have serious processing problems, off-the-charts anxiety, excruciating fear issues, incredible levels of dog or human aggression, unpredictable reactions to stimuli, and on and on.

For them, learning can be close to impossible. Feeling comfortable in their own skin is totally foreign. Their reactions and decisions are often puzzling and unpredictable. Their nervous systems are a wreck. Their aggression, unsettling.

Thankfully they're not the norm, but to not acknowledge that they're out there would be doing owners of these dogs a disservice. To imply that any and every dog can be a safe, reliable, consistent, and comfortable companion is, unfortunately, simply not the case.

P.S. That said, be wary of this diagnosis coming down swiftly and without thorough work and effort from highly experienced folks who deal with this regularly. There are many in the training world who either aren't familiar with serious rehab and don't know what to do with it or feel any dog with issues (who doesn't respond to positive-only methods) should be put down. Be sure to get a 2nd and 3rd opinion from trainers with lots of experience and a varied background of methodology.

theceiling

Whether we want to admit it or not, every dog has one.

It can be incredibly high, or it can be surprisingly low.

With as many dogs as we work with, we're privy to seeing these varying ceilings often. And unfortunately, with dogs whose ceilings are heavily compromised, it can put a cap on progress, abilities, and possibilities, even with great training and the right tools.

Genetic issues, early experience issues, habits practiced for so many years they've become deeply entrenched and second nature.

Nervousness, insecurity, anxiety, reactivity, fear...these are where we see the ceiling most often.

Dogs that struggle, even post-training. Dogs that continue to display their issues, regardless of continued work and exposure.

Can we always be looking to improve and raise that ceiling? Absolutely. Can we consistently push for better and more answers? You bet. But acknowledging that limits exist, limits that sometimes go beyond training, can be a crucial point of acceptance...for you and your dog. 🐾

the art of SEEING THE REAL

I see a lot of people that view dogs in a pretty broad fashion.

A lot of folks see dogs as dogs and their behavior as, well, just being dog-like. They tend to see more of the species in general and less of the individual.

But here's the thing: Dogs are just like us. Of course not in all respects, but in the way that they are very much individuals, with personality and attitudes that vary greatly from dog to dog.

I know lots of folks reading this are saying "of course, we all know dogs are individuals," but what I'm trying to get at is here is something that I don't think gets talked about enough in dog training or dog owning: attitude and demeanor.

Of course, experiences and breed (or mix thereof) play a significant role in shaping who our dogs are and how they respond to the world around them. But I believe they also have hard-wired, fundamental attitude and demeanor differences—not just breed-specific genetics—but individual attitudes. And these attitude and demeanor differences are the filter that all your dog's experiences and choices are processed through.

You can take two dogs and put them in the same challenging environment, and one will become insecure, shy, and avoid confrontation, and the other will become insecure, untrusting, and pursue confrontation. Or you can raise three dogs in the same household with the same rules, and you will find that one dog will always push boundaries more than the others, one will be sweeter, and one will be more aloof or disconnected. Or any other of the millions of behavior and attitude combinations possible.

Why do some dogs become possessive while others could not care less? Why do some easily give way to another dog while another is ready to scrap at the drop of a hat? Once again, I understand that breed, genetics, and experiences all play their part, but I've seen plenty of multi-dog homes with the same breed of dog, from the same breeder, living in the same household, having had almost the exact experiences, with totally different behavior and choices going down with each dog.

And as anyone who has raised kids, or who was a kid in a multi-child household can attest, it's the exact same thing with humans. We all come to the table with our unique attitudes and demeanor, and we apply these attitudes and ways of being to whatever life brings our way. And we all need different approaches to bring out our best.

That's why, if you want to be successful with your dog, training and living wise, it's so important to see your dog as an individual at the deepest level—and not just the cute stuff!

Do you have the pushy brat, who takes that mile every time you accidentally give an inch? Do you have that sweet, soft, super-sensitive dog who with just a raised eyebrow you can stop in his or her tracks? Or do you have the sensitive dog who is also pushy and bratty? That's the tricky part of all this; dogs are rarely all one thing. They're often a multitude of conflicted combinations of attitudes and choices. And many learn—because it's a survival skill—how to manipulate other dogs and people through all sorts of clever behavior, that looks like one thing while it conceals something totally different.

Just like us.

"If you treat dogs as a one-size-fits-all, you're going to find yourself with a lot of bad fits."

Of course, humans and dogs are vastly different, with the differences being easy to see, but the bigger challenge for most folks is seeing the similarities. Not just the cute and easy stuff, but the more nuanced and convoluted stuff. The stuff they, just like us, work so hard to conceal. The true attitude and intent under the behavior.

So the work is to see your dog as an individual at the deepest, most nuanced level. And then, just like the child that needs firmer rules than his brother to succeed, or the child that needs the softer, more well-thought out emotional response to not be overwhelmed, your work is to become the parent that gives that individual the custom-tailored approach he or she needs to be their very best.

Because if you treat dogs as a one-size-fits-all, you're going to find yourself with a lot of bad fits.

camouflage

Many owners never see the nervous, freaked out, highly insecure, and even fearful dog they have.

Why?

Because it's been camouflaged.

It's been camouflaged by your dog through all sorts of other behaviors. Behaviors that often don't look like the true stuff they're feeling underneath.

Instead of the real stuff, owners will often see pulling, zig-zagging, barking, or lunging on walks. In the house, they'll often see excessive barking, pacing, obsessive behavior, growling at guests, major reactivity to anything changing in the environment, possessiveness, dog fights, or bullying in multi-dog households, and more.

Dogs typically channel their nervous, unsure, or fearful energy into movement and action. So you don't see what you would expect to see...until you create stillness and structure.

Once you ask one of these guys to walk in a perfect heel, you'll see it. The structure of the heel reveals the excessive head movements that are used to nervously watch and scan the environment. It reveals the exaggerated jumpiness to sound, movement or objects that used to be concealed by constant motion. It reveals the true concern and worry about other dogs, rather than just the nasty looking reactivity stuff.

And once you ask these guys to be in place or down inside the home—to be still for an extended period of time—you'll see it. The place or down reveals worried, darting eyes and exaggerated nervous reactions to changes in sound and action around the house. It reveals a dog that will often try to break command to run and hide now that it can't bark and explode. And it often reveals a shaking, freaked out, far less confident-looking dog.

And that's the dog. The true dog. Remove that motion and action—the camouflage—and you start to see the true stuff.

---

play a little HARD TO GET

One of the best (and simplest) ways to create a better, more balanced relationship with your dog is to simply play a little hard to get. That doesn't mean ignore or not enjoy your dog; it just means that even your dog knows that things that are always available or too easily obtained aren't as valuable or appreciated. Whether it's a toy that's always out, a food bowl that always has food in it, or affection and attention always on tap, all these things become less special and taken for granted. The only extra wrinkle when it's the human that's too easily obtained is that we present ourselves as needy, soft, and not worthy of listening to. And that can lead to big problems. Instead, hold back a little, make your dog work for your attention and affection. Don't make your dog your love-surrogate. And be aware that doting constantly on your dog creates the same kind of bratty, entitled dog, just as it would with a child.

good work (IF YOUR DOG CAN GET IT)

Dogs always do what 'works' for them.

If pulling on the leash works to get you to walk faster or gets them to a desired tree, they will do it.

If barking from the crate works to get the crate door opened and them out, they will do it.

If acting the fool when you pull the leash out works to get the leash put on, they will do it.

If barking and lunging at other dogs on the walk works to make the other dog go away (the dog's perception) or is just a bunch of fun, they will do it.

If jumping up on you works to get attention (even negative attention), they will do it.

If pulling you out the front door works to get the walk started, they will do it.

If barking at the back door works to get them inside, they will do it.

If whining works to get them petted or soothed, they will do it.

If chewing or mouthing on your pant leg or your hands works to get you to engage with them, they will do it.

If staring or growling at you works to cause you to move away from the food bowl, crate, toy, bed, etc., they will do it.

And they will do all of these things more and more intensely, and more frequently, the more it works for them.

Our job, as our dog's leader and guide, is to be sure that we only encourage the behaviors we like – what 'works' for us and our lifestyle – and discourage that which doesn't work for us.

using FEAR to train owners

"You're going to ruin your relationship."

"You're going to make your dog scared of you."

"You're going to shut your dog down."

"You'll crush his spirit."

"You'll ruin your dog."

"You'll create a ticking time bomb."

Or, my favorite: "Your dog will slide into learned helplessness!" (Love that one!)

These are just a few of the fear-based messages that are lobbied about to try to scare owners away from using certain tools in training (especially prong and E-collars), as well as correcting their dogs for any unwanted or even dangerous behavior. The messages are built around all sorts of super scary outcomes. Ruining your dog or your relationship sounds pretty darn bad. So owners, being good folks and not wanting to ruin their dogs or relationships, try all sorts of methods that will keep things happy, healthy, and "humane."

The problem starts when owners find that these "kinder," "gentler" methods leave their dogs, and themselves stuck. The problem behavior doesn't go away. The jumping, barking, biting, growling, charging, pulling, exploding, guarding, fighting, or running away continues.

In fact, in many cases, it gets worse.

So what's a conscientious and caring owner to do? Educate yourself.

That's truly my best advice. Don't just take these scary messages at face value; instead, do your homework. Dig around and dive into some of the videos and resources out there. Do a Google or YouTube search of E-collar trainers or prong collar trainers. Take responsibility to find out what's really going on out there. You can't be scared into submission if you're educated. Simple as that.

Once you really start getting educated, you'll be able to decide for yourself what you believe. You'll be able to see with your own eyes if these dogs being trained with these tools are being ruined. You'll get to decide if the dogs that were barking, biting, pulling, growling, and freaking out look better, more relaxed, and even happier than they did prior to these evil devices and people coming into their lives. 🐾

There are some pretty amazing answers and approaches out there that can create some pretty fantastic changes in even the most problem dogs. But like anything in life, you gotta search and work hard to find the good stuff. You have to become an informed, conscientious, critical consumer.

So search out the information—compare it, critique it, and draw your own conclusions. Then move forward, confident that you're doing what YOU'VE decided is best!

Few industries have as much contentious, friction-filled, vitriolic, opinionated, near-religious beliefs being flung around as does the dog training world. It's crazy!

People and trainers will noisily (and nastily) condemn the tools, training methods, and approaches being used by others. Whether it's pure positive trainers cursing prong collars, E-collars, and/or any form of correction - or even saying "no" to your dog, or it's "balanced" trainers slinging mud at each other for perceived poor training, or training that doesn't mesh with their beliefs.

That's cool and all, knock yourself out. But all I want is proof.

Don't show scientific studies, or site science-y sounding rhetoric. Don't talk about the hows and whys and benefits of a certain method. Don't offer strongly-felt opinions. Instead, show us! Show us over and over your approach to creating great results—and the owners getting the same results. If you're getting great results, this should be easy enough to do. I know it's work to capture before-and-after footage and to edit it and all. I get it. But if you want your opinion to have any legs, and any chance of being entertained, that's the price of admission today. If you want anyone to listen, to care, to change, to adopt something, simply show us its value. Easy peasy.

Because talk is cheap. Everyone can talk a big game. We all can declare certain tools or approaches to be the worst or the best, but only results matter. Only results are real. Only results walk the talk. Everything else is just the easy part…talk and opinion.

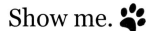

One thing that throws a lot of owners is finding out that their "aggressive," "protective," "possessive," "resource guarding," "bully," is actually a fearful, nervous, insecure, freaked out dog.

Almost every dog that comes through our doors is masking or fronting. They may appear one way, but when that approach is blocked, the mask falls. And when the mask comes off, and the front comes down, we're left with the actual dog.

The dog that was trying to lunge and bite a few minutes ago is now shaking, unsure, head swiveling around nervously. From attacking to... something very different.

Or it might be the dog who's barking, growling, pulling, or lunging

what lies BENEATH

Look deeper.

Look at the attitude and intent of the dog, not just the surface level behavior. That's where you'll find your answers.

at everything on walks. Once that's not allowed, we see that the "aggressive" dog is actually a fearful wreck. Scared of anything and everything.

Why the mask? Why the front?

My personal feeling is that it's primarily a survival tactic. Appearing weak, unsure, or fearful is just too dangerous. And on another level, I think living fearfully is far more uncomfortable than living like a confident bully—even if the confidence is manufactured.

So we get dog after dog who appear to be one thing, but are actually something else altogether. And at this point, we've seen this so often that we expect it. We know once we block the usual coping mechanisms – those habits and patterns of replacing what's really being felt with something more comfortable or easy – we'll start to see the true dog.

And from there, we can actually help.

THE LAUNDRY LIST

Inevitably, when owners bring their dogs to us, they come with a host of complaints and issues...

He pulls on the leash, she jumps on people, he steals stuff off the table, she freaks out at dogs on walks, he's crazy in the car, she's a maniac when guests arrive, he barks out the front window all day, she paces the house and follows me everywhere, he's scared of kids on walks...

And on and on.

We call this "The Laundry List."

We almost never address all these issues directly. Some things, like dog reactivity or pulling, or aggression issues, yeah, we address them head on, but the majority of things on that list just fade away as the overall dog transforms.

It's kind of an amazing thing to watch. As the dog becomes less stressed, less anxious, has fewer options, gets direct communication about what's wanted and not wanted, and is led through life, rather than existing in a leadership vacuum, an amazing amount of symptoms disappear. And that's exactly what so many of these issues are...symptoms.

This is why I rattle on about leadership, structure, rules, and accountability constantly. Because I've watched them transform dog after dog after dog. And because I'm desperate to convey to owners that so many issues they're struggling with are simply symptoms of this leadership vacuum—not issues in and of themselves.

So the mission continues. We'll keep spreading the word, and showing dogs who come in with "The Laundry List" and leaving without it.

How do we get there?

Some simple overall shifts.

We go after the real problem, instead of micro-managing and chasing symptoms of a bigger issue. 🐾

BUT DO YOU REALLY GET IT?

Do you get that affection is a message?

Do you get that freedom is a message?

Do you get that blowing out of the crate or front door is a message?

Do you get that pulling you around on walks is a message?

Do you get that jumping on you or others is a message?

Do you get that barking out the window at dogs or people is a message?

Do you get that sleeping on your bed or the couch is a message?

Do you get that NOT addressing bad behavior or blowing you off is a message?

Do you get that giving your soft stuff to a poorly behaved, disrespectful dog is a message?

Here's the thing; the dog you have will determine if these messages create problems or not, and to what degree. If you've got a sweet, soft, happy-go-lucky, stable dog, you can get away with a lot more of this stuff—often with little to no fallout. If you have a pushy, bratty, anxious, or insecure dog, you'd better be hyper-aware of every one of these messages and what they're saying to your dog about you and your relationship.

Different dogs, different amounts of latitude. Your work is to KNOW which dog you have, and make sure the messages you share work...for both of you.

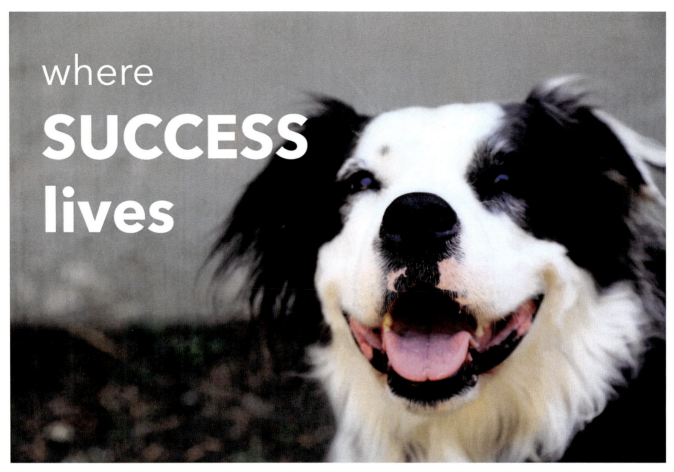

There's lots of talk in dog training circles about owners needing to "become" something better for the training process.

"Become" more calm. "Become" more confident. "Become" more relaxed. "Become" more assertive.

But "becoming" isn't magically produced. It's a by-product of results, a by-product of reality, a by-product of seeing, not preaching.

I've found over and over that when the tools, strategies, and the coaching WORK, meaning something actually changes in the results and behavior of the dog, people can "become" a lot of things. Confidence builds, calm prevails, assertiveness replaces uncertainty.

Owners, when they start to feel safe that these new choices and behaviors will be there when they need them, start to shift automatically, organically. It's a natural by-product of success.

Yes, a great mindset of optimism and belief is definitely a prerequisite. **But mindset alone, without the right tools and training approach to create real results, won't help you or your dog break through.**

turning off AUTO PILOT

One of the most important factors in changing a dog's problem behavior is getting them out of auto-pilot mode.

Auto-pilot mode consists of reacting without thinking. Automatic, deeply patterned habits that tend to get worse and worse. Some typical examples: barking at anything that moves, flying through thresholds (crate, front or back door, car, etc.), reactivity on leash, growling around food or people, jumping up, counter-surfing, whining, and many more.

Basically the dog has learned to experience something—a trigger of any kind—and to have an immediate reaction without the need to process or evaluate what the best choice or reaction would be.

Think of it like you practicing zero impulse control, and zero conscious thought about appropriate behavior, and simply reacting to life. That would look something like: someone honks at you and you run them off the road. Someone looks at you funny and you explode and attack them. Someone is about to park their car in a spot and you see it and race over and try to bully them out of it. You walk up to anyone of the opposite sex and immediately start touching them.

Now I know these are some extreme human examples, but I wanted to illustrate how this process might look in the human world. And the other piece of this is, if allowed to continue, all these unfortunate behaviors you engaged in would likely just worsen. And why not, if there's no consequence for the choice? You'd quickly become a menace to society.

So back to the dogs. When dogs arrive here, we almost always (okay, always!) see dogs on auto-pilot. They drag their owners out of the car, through our gate, in the front door, they pull every direction, they can't sit still, and 90% end up jumping fully onto our coffee table and doing the tap dance we've seen so often (true story!). Once the owners leave, we get the same stuff with food, jamming in or out of the crate, barking just because, etc., etc.

Our first order of business once the dogs are here is reprogramming this simple piece of the dog puzzle. Creating concern for impulse control, conscious thought about their actions, and awareness of consequences for poor choices. Just this process alone creates about 75% of the transformation—eliminating much of the reactivity, stress, anxiety, and silliness.

That's why you always hear me rambling on about thresholds, crate exercises, waiting for food, the immaculate heel, etc. Because I know that if you guys go after that stuff, and get the auto-pilot turned to conscious pilot, you'll be a long way towards your goal of better, happier dogs. And a happier you!

the GIFT of
accountability

We all can do better.

We all can raise our game, make better decisions, and be better versions of ourselves.

But often we fall below what we're capable of.

Why?

When we see we can get away with less, give less, take advantage of more, and push boundaries for an immediate moment of gratification or personal benefit - and we don't see an immediate downside or consequence for the choice or behavior - it's easy to offer less than our best. Less than what we're actually capable of. Yes, even **you**. :)

But then there's the gift of accountability. It's a gift that holds each of us to our best. A gift shared that's says, "I know you're better than this, I know you're capable of more, and for your best and my best, I'm going to hold you to this best."

Whether it's with a co-worker, a family member, a mate, or your dog, when we allow those around us to give less than their best, we rob them, ourselves, and everyone else in their sphere, of the great stuff they're capable of.

And while most of us struggle hard enough with setting boundaries and consequences in the human world, with our dogs it can be even more challenging. They seem like innocents that just do what comes naturally. But the truth is, your dog needs to be held accountable as much as anyone else in your life if they're going to offer their best. Because like us, they'll happily push boundaries, take advantage, and get into trouble if left without consequences or fallout for their choices and behavior.

So a great exercise is to work to look at accountability and consequences in a different fashion. Instead of seeing them as punitive or demanding or mean, see them for what they truly are, a gift. A gift you give to help someone else (and yourself) be their very best.

if your dog **owns the house...**

Unlike what they say about Vegas, what happens in the house doesn't stay in the house.

The attitude, behavior, and relationship you cultivate in your home will undoubtedly rear its head in other places— and the walk, where your dog tends to be most excited, intense, or stressed, is the perfect place to see the results of what's really going on in your life and relationship.

All the moments with your dog stack.

The moment your dog goes to pull to a tree on a walk and you either correct that pulling or allow it.

The moment your dog barks demandingly from the crate and you either correct it or allow it.

The moment your dog tries to excitedly pull through the threshold and you either correct it or allow it.

The moment your dog growls or barks at someone walking by your living room window and you either correct it or allow it.

The moment your dog jumps on you and you either correct it or allow it.

The moment your dog ignores your recall command and you either correct it or allow it.

STACKING the MOMENTS

All these moments stack. They might seem inconsequential, nit-picky, and not-that-big-of-a-deal, but I guarantee you they're all stacking. And by stacking I mean they're repeatedly giving your dog information in teeny bite-sized pieces about who you are in the relationship. About whether rules are to be regarded or disregarded. About whether your dog needs to offer his best stuff or his easiest stuff.

And they either lead your dog's attitude and state of mind in a direction of polite, responsive and respectful, OR pushy, entitled, and bratty.

Like everything else in life, the small, seemingly unimportant moments stack up, and they stack up big! But because they're so small, and because in the moment they seem so insignificant, we can easily fall victim to letting them slide. But drip by drip, teeny choice by teeny choice, we're teaching and guiding and moving our dogs in a direction.

But which direction is the question?

Understanding this stacking concept at a deep level—and realizing that the little moments with your dog not only matter but that they're actually the BIG moments—will set you up to understand and create the same transformations that even us dog trainers are able to create.

why all the crazy?

So what causes all this on-leash reactivity with our dogs?

While there's no perfect answer that covers every individual dog, there are a few reasons that tend to be the most common causes for most dogs. The two biggies are fear and excitement.

The first camp is the fearful or insecure dogs. They know they're on a leash and are, for all intents and purposes, trapped. That trapped feeling causes many fearful or insecure dogs to panic. They may just freak out because they're overwhelmed, or they might freak out in order to try to keep the other dog away. Either way, it looks scary and aggressive.

The second camp is the excited, and often bratty dogs. They like dogs...a lot. They see dogs and want to go play and say "hi." The leash prevents them from doing so, so you'll often get bratty explosions of disagreement...which often look like aggression.

Of course, you can also get those conflicted dogs. The ones that are nervous and curious and bratty. They'll keep you guessing. :)

A couple of honorable mentions go to these other triggers. We don't see them nearly as often, but we do see them from time to time. These are territorial issues in the dog's 'hood, and possessive issues around their owners.

The good news is the answer, for any of the above, is the same. We don't change our approach whether it's fear based or excitement based. Keep it simple. All of the above dogs are listening to their impulses and acting out inappropriately...yes, even the fearful ones. The approach is to use the best tools, create an immaculate heel, and correct any inappropriate choices (staring, loading, barking, speeding up, lunging, etc.)

Whether bratty, fearful, territorial, or possessive, they're all unhealthy, poor choices. They all lead the dogs to continued bad behavior that will likely just get worse. Take charge and lead these dogs. Make the bad choices uncomfortable and the good ones comfortable.

Do all this and watch the issues, regardless of where they originate from emotionally, transform.

P.S. Many of these dogs, when off leash, and allowed the freedom to move freely, to comfortably engage or not, and to do their thing as they wish, will behave completely differently. Many on-leash aggression cases are completely non-existent when that leash comes off.

Just because your dog has been practicing bad habits for months or years doesn't mean you're stuck.

Even serious, long-standing issues can be massively changed if not completely resolved.

That "old dog, new trick" fairy tale is just that...

A fairy tale.

what you PET is what you GET.

Want a bratty dog?
Pet a bratty dog.

Want a nervous dog?
Pet a nervous dog.

Want a fearful dog?
Pet a fearful dog.

Want a possessive dog?
Pet a possessive dog.

Want an aggressive dog?
Pet an aggressive dog.

"Dogs are eager to please... themselves."

"If you really look, if you really dig deep, if you really deconstruct your dog's choices, you'll see at the heart of every choice (even the ones that seem so loving and sweet) is a payoff for your dog."

Something I see a lot of is female owner and male dog struggles.

A lot.

Now, this doesn't mean that there aren't tons of exceptions - females with male dogs that are angels, and female owners with female dogs that are incredibly challenging - there are these exceptions. But that doesn't change the fact that, if I'm super honest, I see far more of the former than the latter.

There are so many factors that go into this, but the biggies, in my opinion and experience, are that females naturally tend to gravitate towards more nurturing and loving behavior, and males tend to gravitate towards more assertive, domineering, and protective behavior.

Yes, these are giant generalizations. Yes, there are female owners who are way tougher, more assertive than their male spouses, and male spouses that are super nurturing and much softer than their female counterparts. Totally. But we're talking about overall trends, rather than exceptions.

So what happens when you put a super nurturing, soft, loving female owner with an assertive, protective, pushy male dog? Often what you get is overly protective, hyper-territorial, possessive, mine-mine-mine domineering behavior.

The soft female energy that also is the giver of food, affection, fun, love, comfort, etc., becomes something to protect, guard, and often take advantage of. The lack of strong boundaries, strong rules, and believable, strong energy (as perceived by the dog) becomes a terrific imbalance, and something that leaves both dog and human in the lurch.

Many of these dogs become the typical overly-possessive boyfriend. The demanding and overbearing (and insecure) dude that sees everyone as a threat. That sees you as his "old lady." :)

This lack of balance between the sexes makes for stressed out dogs and lots of terrible behavior. The good intentions of caring and loving (without appropriate and commensurate boundaries) are misconstrued as stuff to be taken advantage of, and stuff to be possessed or owned.

The trick isn't for female owners to not have male dogs. Lots of female owners have very successful relationships with their male dogs. The trick is to see the possible dynamic, understand that it's actually in play, and then ensure that you balance out your relationship. Set boundaries and rules that are as firm and strong as your love and affection.

Remember that, regardless of sex, your job is still the same: to lead, guide, and be the rock for your dog—not the reverse.

WHEN DID LEADING BECOME A DIRTY WORD?

When did being in charge, showing the way, using experience, wisdom, and insights your dog isn't privy to, to help them succeed, become a bad thing?

When I adopted Watson in January of 2014, I had no idea what I was getting myself into.

I remember the first night home he growled at me, it terrified me, but I wrote it off as him being stressed from the 9-hour drive home from the rescue, and being in a new environment…

I was wrong.

As the months went on, Watson's aggression and insecurities continued to progress. Due to my failing to provide the structure he needed, Watson took it upon himself to guard not only our house but me as well. He growled, lunged, and nipped at more than one guest that we had over.

He was eventually not allowed to be out when people were over, but that led to him clawing at and destroying several doors. Additionally, Watson decided that he didn't like people getting near me, even family members. This resulted in my sister and mom being afraid of Watson and him not being welcome at my parents' house. Watson showed insecurities in everything he did. He was constantly pacing and monitoring everyone in the house and never relaxed on our daily walks.

Our walks were fine…as long as we didn't pass other dogs. If we passed a dog that was pulling, or showing any interest in Watson, it led to lunging and barking. I worked with 3 different trainers over a year and wasted thousands of dollars. These trainers ensured me that if I gave Watson treats when he saw a dog or when we had people over that it would condition him that these were positive experiences. This could not have been further from the truth.

Watson's aggression escalated and one by one each trainer told me that Watson was beyond repair and one even suggested euthanasia.

Things reached an all-time low on Thanksgiving Day in 2015. Watson was anxious because my entire family was home and I think that he could tell that we were preparing to leave the house. He went and hid under the kitchen table, which led to me talking to him and trying to get him to come so that I could put him in his crate. He had his head down and would not make eye contact and when I went to grab his collar to lead him to his crate, he freaked out and started attacking me. After many tearful days and deep pondering, I contacted the rescue where I had gotten Watson and told them that I would be returning him. I had been able to keep everyone safe up to this point by keeping Watson away from people or having him muzzled, but I knew that I couldn't keep a dog that was going to attack me.

When word got around at the rescue that Watson was being returned, I was contacted by a woman that is a balanced trainer. She told me that this sounded like a case for Sean and asked if I would check out the website before making my final decision. That night I started watching the before and after videos on The Good Dog site and was in awe of the results they were achieving. Maybe these trainers really could help Watson. I was hesitant and was mentally prepared for failing once again, but I decided to give this one last trainer a try.

Watson participated in the three-week board and train and the results were amazing. The Good Dog did an amazing job doing the initial training and explained things to me at the go home session in a manner that made learning how to work with Watson easy. Even upon pick-up and seeing this new side of Watson I was still nervous and hesitant. But upon bringing Watson home, I witnessed a different side of him, a much more relaxed Watson. It was like a huge weight had been lifted off of his shoulders and I saw a more chill, fun loving, relaxed dog.

Where before he would be pacing and patrolling, he was now content staying in "place" and allowing me to take control. I was worried that this would change who Watson fundamentally was, but it allowed his true personality to develop and emerge. Although The Good Dog did all of the heavy lifting as far as training Watson, it became quite apparent early on that if I did not keep up on my end of the deal that he could very easily slip back into his old ways, so I have been diligent about working hard to ensure that Watson stays in this carefree, happy mindset.

Training Watson has become my favorite hobby. We are often complimented on his excellent behavior and his calm demeanor. Our walks are now stress free and enjoyable. It is such a comfort knowing that I can put him on "place" and have him stay there no matter the circumstances around him. Not only did Watson's behavior change, but I can tell that he is in a much healthier place mentally, as well. Working with The Good Dog taught me so much and allowed me to become his advocate, which included providing the structure and guidance that Watson needed to succeed and live a safe, happy, mentally healthy life.

WATSON

PLAYING HARD TO GET

A big issue-creator we see between dogs and owners is when owners simply try too hard.

They're too desperate to connect, and they end up pushing constantly for more emotional and physical contact.

This creates relationship dynamics that are super unhealthy. Dogs feel pressured and uncomfortable. Dogs feel owners supplicating and needy. Dogs become annoyed, disrespectful, suspicious of intent...and entitled brats.

This is the road to relationship ruin.

Of course, whenever we try too hard, it's always an indication of our own needs, our own gaps. And in the same way that we see that in other humans, and feel the discomfort that goes with it, so do our dogs.

Owners that need their dogs far too much try too hard, and that are always moving towards their dogs for more closeness and bonding, often end up creating the exact opposite.

An easy way to think about how to improve your relationship with your dog, if it needs improving, is to simply play hard to get. Be slightly aloof. Don't need your dog so much. Let them come to you. Let them desire an interaction rather than be constantly subjected to it.

As they say, absence makes the heart grow fonder. And distance—emotional and physical—creates desire from your dog for more. It draws your dog to you. It also sets up a healthy dynamic of a balanced relationship. One in which your dog doesn't see a needy person, desperate for contact and connection, but instead sees a person of value. One that they want to interact more with, and especially, one worthy of listening to, following, and respecting.

We humans don't follow, respect, or enjoy the overly needy, so don't be surprised that your dog feels the same way.

Play a little hard to get and see what shifts you see in your dog and your relationship. It's what we do all day long in the training world, and it works like a charm.

MAGIC WORDS!

This can be a funny one, I don't mean to be mean or snarky, it's just a quick reality check. :)

I hear lots of folks using words like "heel," "leave-it," "no," "settle" etc. All great stuff, but they're usually being used like magic. Meaning, words that have magic abilities in and of themselves to communicate, control, and change dog behavior.

But here's the thing—until you teach your dog the meaning of a word and the corresponding behavior that goes along with it, and then proof it with compliance/corrections, these words have no meaning.

Zero, zip, nada.

You might as well use "broccoli" to get your dog to slow down and walk next to you. Or you could try "shazam," or "right-on" to get your dog to stop trying to attack other dogs on leash, or jumping on people.

Just remember, there's no magic in these words until you put it in them. Once you actually train your dog what the commands mean, then you can actually communicate and make some magic happen.

IF YOU'VE GOT **GREAT KIDS**

There's always lots of flack flying around from us dog trainers about not babying your dogs.

And that's solid advice. Babies don't have rules; they don't get disciplined, they aren't asked to do their best work. They're just babies. They're loved on, allowed to do whatever they need/want to do, and we don't ask anything of them.

Now kids, on the on other hand, are a whole different story. Kids have rules. Kids have structure. Kids are accountable for their behavior and are disciplined for breaking known rules and misbehaving. Kids are loved on, yes, they're perhaps even doted on, but if they're in a healthy family, they're also kept in balance with parental leadership, rules, and accountability.

It's not that being your dog's mom or dad is the problem. It's not. If you're being a balanced parent to your dog, sharing leadership, structure, rules, and accountability, along with all the fun and affectionate stuff, then "mom" and "dad" away!!

The problem is when we treat our dogs like babies, and we behave like parents of infants. When we view our dogs as infants or babies—creatures that only require love, affection, fun, and caretaking—that's where it gets sticky. And that's usually when you come and see us.

The upshot is this: People who understand the dynamics of great parenting—whether they have kids or not—are going to be successful with their dogs. This stuff isn't all that crazy or complex. We've just gotten away from common sense. We've been programmed to view kids and dogs as equals that need "friends" or "buddies" that need to be negotiated with and bribed into good behavior.

But when kids and dogs are denied the dependability and comfort that goes along with strong, confident, non-negotiable leadership (or parenting), we see them stumble. Instead of offering us their best, we get their easiest. Instead of them offering their respect, we get their disdain. Instead of them feeling confident and secure, we see anxious, worried, insecure, and often bratty behavior. When no one is in charge, everything is up for grabs. And when everything is up for grabs, it means you haven't done your job.

Instead, be clear, be confident, be resolute. Own your decisions and your responsibility. Be prepared to be met with friction and resentment. Know that good parenting isn't about always being popular, and it isn't supposed to be a party 24/7. Neither is raising a dog.

So if you've got great kids, rejoice, because you already know the secret. And you'll probably say this secret isn't that complex or difficult. It's about giving kids what they truly need, even when it's hard, even when it's uncomfortable. Actually, especially when it's hard and especially when it's uncomfortable.

Same goes with your dog. 🐾

> **If your dog is your kid, make sure you're an amazing parent!**
>
> Amazing parents hold their children to a high standard of behavior. Amazing parents have non-negotiable rules. Amazing parents create dependable structure to make their kids feel safe. Amazing parents are willing to make difficult decisions and be the heavy when needed. Amazing parents recognize that someone has to be in charge, and if they won't be, then their kids suffer. Amazing parents put their kids needs before their personal comfort. Amazing parents understand that all of the above leads to well-adjusted kids...and dogs.

part TWO
the mistakes

the HARDEST thing

What's one of the hardest things for both owners and trainers?

It's the power of association, emotional habits, perceptions, and feelings. All the stuff owners have accidentally or inadvertently created between their dogs, themselves, and their environments.

Watching well-trained, calm, and obedient dogs literally become different animals—reactive, aggressive, crazed, freaked out, incapable of listening, etc.—right before your eyes as the owner enters the room, grabs the leash, or returns the dog home is something that never ceases to amaze and confound.

It's the one thing we can't control. Even with owners doing their homework, having the tools and commands down pat, and showing up ready to change it all, it's still the wildcard in play.

For many dogs it's a seamless transition—they jump right into the new game. For others, it's a totally different story. These dogs are so affected by the relationship, associations, and feelings they have with their owners that their minds and nervous systems simply melt down.

They are so aroused, excited, overwhelmed, over-stimulated, and most of all, reconnected to their past feelings (dependency, guarding, fear, anxiety, excitement, possessiveness, etc.) that they're completely different dogs. They don't respond to commands. They don't care about the tools. They react when they didn't react. They explode when they previously didn't care. The just-minutes-ago calm, well-mannered dog disappears in an instant! They actually engage in physical tics and behaviors (rolling on the ground, scratching, licking, spinning, whining, etc) to try to channel out some of this toxic remembrance and association.

This is the power of relationship and association.

Dogs not only get into behavioral patterns, they also get into emotional and physiological stress patterns. They actually feel emotionally different and physically different around their owners and environments. It's not just about training new

> There's always a way. It's up to you to find it.

behaviors and habits, we have to actually reprogram the emotions and nervous systems of these dogs.

To be successful, these dogs need to actually FEEL different in their owner's presence and in their home environments. They need to be emotionally re-patterned and re-programmed. They need to develop new feelings, new habits, and new associations. This is the mountain that has to be climbed, and the changes that need to be made, if owners in this situation want their dogs to be safe, relaxed, and well-behaved.

These owners have a level of work ahead of them that exceeds the norm. It's not your usual dog training hand over; it's human-and-dog relationship reboot time. World Series version.

For owners who find themselves in this position, I can tell you that what you want is definitely possible, but it can be a long, hard road. Only those who want it bad enough, and who are willing to put in the work, the patience, and the self-reflection needed, will get there.

Hard stuff, for sure, but enormously rewarding.

So much of what we see with problem dogs, and their behavior, is that people have unintentionally reinforced and encouraged the wrong stuff. It's easy to do and easy to misunderstand.

So here's a little list of reminders that we'll call the "don't do," or "watch out for" list. Keeping these in mind and doing your very best to avoid these common dog/owner traps will go a long way towards you having a great relationship and enjoyable life with your dog.

• Trying to love a badly-behaved dog better.

• Coddling, nurturing, babying an insecure, nervous dog.

• Allowing a dog to have constant access to you and your personal space – following you everywhere, jumping in your lap uninvited, always needing to be near.

• Constantly petting a dog.

• Ignoring bad behavior—jumping, whining, barking, fence fighting, growling etc.—in the hopes it will go away.

• Using your dog to fill emotional gaps in your life.

• Not enforcing rules because you feel bad.

• Letting dogs be "dogs"–rationalizing that growling, protective behavior, resource guarding, reactivity etc. is normal or acceptable.

• Being inconsistent with rules and consequences.

• Accidentally rewarding whining, barking, or growling by petting, talking to, or letting in or out of a door or crate.

• Spoiling or allowing bad behavior due to guilt.

• Letting stressed, pulling, anxious, worked up dogs meet on leash.

• Letting dogs pull to trees or bushes on walks.

• Touching, talking to, or "enjoying" a dog who jumps on you.

• Letting dogs "work it out" on their own.

- Giving treats or petting a growling, barking, anxious, or stressed dog to calm and soothe them.

- Sharing only your soft, sweet, loving, affectionate side.

- Using tools that allow dogs to ignore you and the tool.

- Using tools that allow or encourage the dog to behave worse.

- Seeing freedom, love, and affection as more vital to your dog's well-being than structure, rules, and guidance.

- Thinking exercise and activity create calm, relaxed dogs on their own.

- Wanting to be your dog's best friend before having become his leader.

- Thinking dogs just want to please you.

- Not sharing valuable consequences for bad behavior.

- Being afraid that consequences and discipline will ruin your relationship.

- Letting love blind you to your dog's actual needs.

- Letting your needs blind you to your dog's actual needs.

the gift of NO

C'mon guys, how did we let such simple stuff get so complicated and confusing?

How did we allow ourselves to get so bamboozled? How did eternal truths—truths we all are intimately familiar with—become so foreign?

How did saying "no" become so hard?

And just to be clear, when I say to say "no," I'm not talking about the verbal version. I'm talking about giving clear information about what is and isn't okay. I'm talking about consequences, both positive and negative.

Somewhere along the line, sharing both kinds of consequences, saying "yes" and "no," and giving clarity to our dogs became a bad thing. We allowed ourselves to buy into a belief system, an ideology, that punishing bad, dangerous, or unwanted behavior was something old school. It was something that new, more evolved, "science-based" training approaches had proven to be not only unnecessary but actually harmful.

So with this new and improved approach, we were taught to just say "yes." We were taught that dogs learned best through giving lots of "yes" information, and zero "no" information. We were taught that the best approach to a happy, healthy, well-behaved dog was through rewarding the good and ignoring the bad.

If we reinforced what we wanted enough, we'd get exactly what we want. And we wouldn't have to subject our dogs to any of those nasty negative consequences.

What a cool approach, right?

Except for that little part about only giving our dogs half the information they need to succeed.

That little part that robs our dogs of clarity. That little part that creates a foggy game of "guess what you're supposed to do and not do?" rather than clearly spelling it out. That little part about hijacking nature's eternal way of teaching all of us how to best survive and thrive.

And that little part of you that, deep down, always knew better. (But more on that later.)

The main reason dogs end up here with us is that they simply haven't been given both sides of the coin. All of the information. They've been loved, they've been allowed, they've been rewarded, they've been reinforced...but they haven't had any real "no's."

Owners either haven't known how to say "no," haven't been uncomfortable with saying "no," or haven't felt it was okay conceptually to say "no."

So the growling, the jumping, the guarding, the reactivity, the possessiveness, the barking, the biting just continues. And in fact, like anything practiced repeatedly, it actually gets worse and worse.

What ends up happening is, by not saying "no," by not sharing consequences or punishing problem behavior, you actually say "yes" to it. By allowing it, you're reinforcing it through repetition.

So even though the goal was to make our dogs happy, healthy, and well-behaved, we've ended up with something very different. We've ended up with dogs that are a mess.

And how did we get here? By omission. By removing an enormous and crucial piece of our communication. By believing that some ideologically-backed "science" concepts know better than an eternity of nature.

And that's where your culpability comes in. C'mon folks, we're all on this same ship together. We all know what has taught and formed us. We've all witnessed consequences in action. We've personally seen and felt them. We've known all along if we've cared to look honestly enough, that it's precisely these consequences—both positive and negative—that have guided and formed us all.

Can you imagine it being otherwise? Can you imagine trying to make sense of this world if all you got was "yes"? If no one or no thing ever gave you a "no"?

Can you imagine your boss only saying "yes" and never "no"? Can you imagine your college professor only saying "yes" and never "no"? Can you imagine your parents only saying "yes" and never "no?"

Can you imagine how much harder, painful, and more confusing life would have been?

Nature has had this stuff figured out pretty well, for quite some time now. And it's seemed to work pretty darn well. But then here we come.

We've got emotional challenges with sharing negative consequences (we've become soft). We've got a lack of understanding of how to best share negative consequences (we don't know how). And we've got folks saying they've figured out a better way…a way that doesn't require negative consequences (we've allowed ourselves to be bamboozled).

To be honest, if you're connected to reality, dog training is pretty simple stuff. If you follow nature, if you follow how we've all been taught, how life has always taught, you'll realize how straightforward this all is. With a little distance and objectivity, you'll see it really is simple. We've just made it hard…

On us and our dogs.

The good news is if we'll reconnect to nature and simplicity, and if we'll work to reflect the reality and truths we've all been formed by, we can turn this all around. We can use this simple blueprint that has been passed down for millions of years; we can jump back on track.

Life shares "yes" and "no" for a reason.

You should too.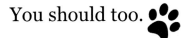

Many folks confuse the state of arousal with excitement, happiness, or a dog being a dog.

But arousal, when you're trying to get your dog to make his best choices, is usually the enemy.

Of course, arousal and excitement do have their places. Play and fun time, or high action work like frisbee, fetch, etc. are all great times for letting it all hang out. Just make sure you have both worlds to offer your dog.

Here's an analogy: A perfectly nice couple of guys go the football game on Sunday. These guys have nice jobs, nice families, are well-respected, and well-liked. Good people. Once they get on the road to the game they start to get excited. They pump some loud music, start talking a little louder and are getting excited about the game. They both notice the little lift they're feeling. Almost a little high, a little carefree, a little (*just a little*) I-don't-give-a-damn attitude creeping

arousal
is the
ENEMY

in. It feels good and a teeny bit dangerous. *But just a teeny bit.*

They arrive at the game, grab their seats, and are swept up in the energy of the crowd and the anticipation of the game.

And then, kickoff!

Boom! The adrenaline starts to flow. Our calm, cool, family men's voices become louder and more intense. Next thing you know, they're pumping their fists and standing up to cheer and shout. Our boys are getting swept up in the moment.

Next thing you know, someone in front of our guys says something inappropriate. It isn't directed at them, it's just a general silly outburst, but due to all the excitement and arousal our guys are feeling, their better judgment lapses for just a moment. One of them shouts back at the offending party. It doesn't take long for things to escalate. A shouting match ensues, and soon enough, an actual physical altercation.

Security arrives to break things up. No one is seriously injured, but the whole thing is pretty ugly. Security escorts our guys and the other man away. Next up, a hot date with the police.

Now how did we get here? How did our nice, respectable, good guys end up making such bad choices, getting themselves in so much trouble? Arousal. They didn't even see it coming. It was like a slow storm that gradually enveloped them and next thing they knew they were **acting like they wouldn't normally act, talking like they wouldn't normally talk, and getting into behavior that they wouldn't normally get into.**

It's the same with our dogs.

Only our dogs don't have the same social pressure we do to comport ourselves in a certain fashion. And they tend to move into this space of arousal much more quickly. We humans tend to need more ammo and time to get lifted up, but our dogs are often on a hair-trigger. They only need a little push to go Boom! And many of our dogs live just on the outskirts of a mild state of arousal most of their lives, so pushing them into a higher state is very easy.

This is why we focus so much on calming exercises like the structured walk, thresholds, crate, duration place, and down. We're looking to cultivate a state of mind that is able to handle excitement and stimulation without boiling over. We teach the dog how to be in an exciting situation and still hold it together. This is a skill set that many owners AND trainers miss. They focus on action, motion, and excitement. And they end up with dogs whose minds only have one gear.

What we're shooting for is much more than just awesome obedience work, we're looking to create a mental landscape that can access calm whenever needed. A dog that has this ability is a dog that will be able to make great choices, share their best behavior, and be their best selves, without needing constant supervision or management. Eventually, it becomes the default.

Once again, this isn't to say this is the ONLY state we want our dogs in; we want them to be able to romp and play and be silly dogs too. They just need both sides of the coin. And the calm side is always the hardest to attain.

Remember, all those dogs you see on walks that are pulling, barking, spinning, lunging, biting the leash…or the dogs in the house that bark, charge, and freak out at anything and everything that moves or makes a sound…they're all just like our dudes at the football game. They're stuck on the arousal merry-go-round. They're at the never-ending game.

Let's help them visit arousal when we want it, and leave it when we don't.

the **WORLD SERIES** of dog training

You don't start swinging the bat the day of the World Series.

You don't throw your first Shot Put the day of the Olympics.

You don't sit down at the piano for the first time the day of your recital at Lincoln Center.

Of course all of these examples are silly, and no one in their right mind would actually contemplate them. BUT, as crazy as these examples are, this is exactly what I see so many dog owners do. And it's one of the biggest causes of failure in their attempts to successfully train or rehabilitate their dog. It's fascinating that something that we so intuitively understand in the human world—the necessity of using baby steps and constant preparation in order to achieve a bigger goal or accomplishment—regularly escapes us and frequently sabotages our attempts to train our dogs.

We somehow believe that the dog with the maniacal door and stranger reaction will remain in place or down, the day that our out-of-state friend arrives. Even without practice or working on the problem in the weeks preceding.

Or, we let our dogs wander and pull on the walk. Zigging and zagging, sniffing and marking wherever they please—teaching them over and over to ignore us and do whatever they want. Then our dog sees that obnoxious little dog from down the street, and strangely enough, instead of listening to our pleas to "Leave-it!", decides to explode!

Both of these are great examples of impractical, unrealistic expectations. These are World Series moments, and you haven't spent any time preparing, practicing, and patterning for the big day. It's no surprise you and your dog lose.

If you're looking to overcome any training or behavior challenges, you have to get to work long before game day. Wishing or wanting ain't gonna get it. You have to condition both you and your dog with tons of repetition and small, incremental challenges that slowly build to bigger accomplishments...long before you actually need them.

It's this slow, incremental, consistent patterning approach that fuels much of our success here at TGD. You can use the same simple approach for equally awesome results with your dog. And if you're unsure of how it works, just look at how you've learned any skill or talent. :)

DUMB DOGS?

Owners are constantly asking if we think their dog is smart enough to learn and excel at training.

Smarts are rarely the issue.

But so many dogs appear "not smart," or tuned-out, or unable to retain what's been taught over and over. It seems like the there's a learning problem, but that's rarely the case.

So what is the problem? Attitude, demeanor, and priorities.

If you haven't created the proper relationship, built on respect, polite behavior, and caring about humans, you'll likely have a dog with an aloof attitude, a bratty demeanor, and priorities that lie elsewhere.

And if all that negative stuff is in place, your very smart dog is going to appear…dumb. It won't be because he doesn't get it, it'll be because he chooses not to. It won't be because he's overwhelmed, it'll be because he's underwhelmed by you. It won't be an intelligence issue. It'll be a priorities issue.

There are very few dogs not equipped to be well-mannered, well-trained dogs, but there are an awful lot of them that might appear that way.

if you don't say **NO**, you're saying
YES...

Remember, whatever is allowed is being trained.

If you don't disagree or correct problem behavior, you're training problem behavior. It's just that simple.

Whether it's jumping, mouthing, pulling, barking, leash reactivity, growling, guarding...you have to say no to what you don't want if you want it to change.

Because stopping the behavior is the first step towards creating new, better, more healthy behavior.

"Your goal should be a dog with a great attitude, **not just a dog with great obedience.**"

a few reminders:

If you can't stop the worst, you certainly can't build the best.

The dogs that most need our strength are usually the ones who get the least of it.

Dogs aren't glass. They won't break. Stop treating them as if they're so fragile.

Respect is the gateway to trust.

Dogs aren't superheroes. Don't ask them to do things and accept things that are beyond their abilities.

Affection doesn't make weak dogs stronger; it makes weak dogs weaker.

Don't be soft with a firm dog.

just RELAX

What if a correction actually felt good? What if a correction was something that helped a dog calm down and relax?

Over and over I've watched correctly applied and timed corrections do just that.

I actually will refer to the button on the E-collar as a "relaxation button." (This can also be applied to a prong collar correction as well.) And while I don't say this to bamboozle owners into feeling better about correcting (even though it is a good perspective changer!), I share it because it's what I've seen...over and over.

I've watched worked up, tense, worried, overwhelmed, scared, fixated, escalating dogs, after a correction, relax. I've watched their body language relax, I've watched their state of mind relax, I've watched the dog calm down and become comfortable again.

It's a hard concept for many to grasp, but once you've seen it in action, you'll realize that the right correction can work wonders, in a positive, helpful, healthy, and relaxing way.

DUKE

My husband Jason and I adopted Duke, a deaf American Pit Bull Terrier, when he was about 4 months old. We were unaware of his deafness at the time, and as soon as he came home...

He was a monster.

He was going to the bathroom in the house, counter surfing, breaking out of his crate, and chewing everything in sight. About two months after we got Duke, a new behavior surfaced:

He began growling and shaking while eating, and would not let us near his bowl.

After a few weeks of the growling and shaking, Duke began attacking our adult APBT mix, Kaya, during feeding time and even hours after—he would remain in a heightened state that we could not get him out of. We had to crate him for hours after the feedings to avoid dog fights.

Duke then began to turn on us if we were in the same room as him during feeding time.

He would literally charge at us in an attempt to get us away from his food.

He then began to attack Kaya over the scent of human food, like if we were eating or cooking dinner. He also began guarding his water bowl and guarding and attacking over high-value toys such as rawhides, and even bit me pretty badly on the hand when I tried to pick up his rawhide.

We did not want to return him to the shelter because we knew that a deaf, aggressive dog would be euthanized. After being bitten, we called a local, highly recommended trainer to begin helping us with Duke's issues. We were beginning to see some progress on his household behavior issues, but Duke was only making good choices when we were in the same room as him. He continued with all behaviors when we were not around, and we had seen no progress with his aggression.

After breaking up dog fights each night for almost two weeks we had decided if Duke couldn't change dramatically and permanently, we would have to return him. At this point we sent an email to The Good Dog, and it was the best decision we could have made for our dog and family.

Duke spent four weeks at The Good Dog. At first, I was hesitant to use the E-collar because I felt it would hurt him, but after observing Duke at TGD, I realized that it is a communicative, not a punitive, tool. We learned the importance of consistency, and of clearly and effectively communicating our intentions with him.

When Duke returned, our work with him began.

We strictly followed the suggested protocol from TGD for two months. It was work on our part for sure, but we were determined to ensure Duke remained the well-mannered pup he was when he was returned to us. We have had him back for a year without incident. He even lets us pet him while eating now, and eats within close proximity of Kaya without incident. Through creating structure and patterns, Duke has truly learned to make good choices whether we are present or not. We even implemented foundations and began using an E-collar for Kaya, who was formerly dog aggressive with any dog larger than her who she was unfamiliar with. She now spends full days at the dog beach without incident.

The significance of having a foundations program and an effective tool to communicate with our dogs has made such an impact in all our lives, and has literally saved Duke's life!

LEVERAGING

What is leverage?

In this context it means **doing smaller, easier things to make doing bigger, harder things easier**.

For example, the hardest place to get your reactive dog to not be reactive is around another dog. That's the big, hard stuff.

So, the first place you look to start fixing dog reactivity is in creating impulse control, respect, and calm behavior. Trying to manufacture this instantaneously around dogs on a walk is a losing proposition. But, if you use the crate exercise just right—allowing your dog to make a choice of waiting calmly, or bolting and being corrected with the crate door—you'll de-escalate him, create impulse control, and a respectful attitude. Nice.

Now we've got a little leverage.

Next, you refuse to leash up a revved up, hyper dog. He has to calm down, practice impulse control, and be respectful in order to get leashed and out.

More leverage.

Now you go to your front door and allow your dog to make a decision: wait calmly or bolt out. Just like the crate. Only this time, bolting gets a firm correction with a prong or E-collar. Repeat this exercise until you have calm, respectful, impulse-control-rich behavior.

More leverage.

Finally, you're on the walk. You demand your dog walks in an immaculate heel, with no sniffing, marking, pulling etc. If he pulls he's corrected, and your dog learns the only comfortable place to walk is right next to you in a heel position. Even though he wants to be doing all sorts of other stuff, he listens to you. Once again we have impulse control with calm, respectful behavior.

More leverage!

What's been happening is that you've been cultivating a relationship (respectful and looking to you for permission), an understanding of acceptable behavior (you've established clear rules and consequences for breaking them), and a state of mind (much calmer, less amped and aroused, which means far better able to make good decisions) - all simultaneously. Massive leverage.

You've now set up you and your dog (if you're using the right tools and techniques) to win. Instead of trying to take on that dog reactivity issue head-on, in its worst and most powerful state, you've instead chipped away at it and created tons of leverage to ensure you've got the very best chance of a successful outcome.

Understanding leverage is almost like magic. It's a game changer when applied correctly, and when all the pieces are executed just right. So focus more on your pre-game being super tight and amazing, and less on the actual big problem moment, and you'll probably find that the actual moment you're most concerned about isn't the big moment it used to be.

Just like magic. 🐾

If you don't say "No", how do they know?

Often, the only thing that stands between good choices and bad choices, good behavior and unsavory behavior, is clearly telling your dog what you want and what you don't want. Simply saying "No" in a way that resonates with your dog can change everything.

Because if you don't clearly tell them what you want, **how are they supposed to know?**

*I don't mean a verbal "No," I mean a valuable consequence!

tradition, aesthetics, and **getting fancy**

If there are three things we don't prioritize at TGD, it's the list to the left.

For me, I've always felt that these were hindrances to growth, open-mindedness, and finding the very best solutions.

If you're concerned about tradition, you'll probably overlook (or consciously dismiss) that cool but unorthodox training idea you just had. If you're concerned with aesthetics, you definitely won't be down with a quiet, relaxed dog who behaves awesomely but doesn't look like he's on high alert when doing commands. If you're concerned about fancy, you'll definitely prioritize appearance (fancy-looking behavior) over substance (true transformation).

At TGD we've worked hard to strip away everything that doesn't lead to a better outcome—even if it means we look a little less fancy. Even if we buck tradition. Even if our aesthetics won't win any awards. Our goal is success in real life—for both dog and owner. Anything that doesn't contribute to that or that impedes that goal gets tossed aside.

But...

That's just us. Our business is primarily behavior modification and training for family dogs. So our goals are centered strictly around what creates the very best outcomes for that work. If you're competing in obedience or doing sport work, that's an entirely different world and an entirely different approach. In that world, tradition, aesthetics, and fancy might just be what the doctor ordered.

For owners looking to make sense of all the different approaches out there in the training world, the trick is to determine what your goals are, and then find the best fit for them. If you want to compete, find a trainer who excels at that. If you want a well-behaved family dog that knows basic commands and manners, find a trainer who excels at that. If you have a dog with behavior issues that you're looking to overcome, find a trainer who excels at that. (In some cases you might just find a trainer who can do some or all of the above extremely well, but that would be a very rare bird. Check them out thoroughly.)

Most importantly, make sure you don't get caught up in thinking the fancy looking stuff equals transformation.

Just because a dog looks good doesn't mean he feels good.

So many dogs with issues tend to automatically get labeled as abused.

Their owners or caretakers often create elaborate stories and possible causes for their fear, insecurity, reluctance, panic, and unique emotional triggering around specific people or things.

And of course, there are abused dogs out there. Of course there are dogs who have seen some really unfortunate stuff, and their behavior might be directly connected to that abuse. But in my experience as a trainer, I see very few true abuse cases and subsequently, far less abuse-related behavior issues.

WHAT DIDN'T HAPPEN
TO YOUR DOG

What do I see more often as the actual root cause of so many behavior problems and struggling dogs?

Usually what I see isn't that some horrible event or trauma has occurred. Usually what I see is either a lack of solid genetics, a lack of exposure, a lack of leadership - or some combination of all three.

Many owners aren't familiar with the crucial role that genetics play in their dog's behavior and abilities. Genetics, to a large degree, determine how able your dog is to adapt to their world; whether they're curious or terrified, emotionally strong or weak, and how resilient they are to experiences. Dogs with compromised genetics will often be skittish and fearful. They'll cower, shake, and show uncomfortable body language. These dogs often get labeled as abused, but they're simply dealing with genetics that are working against them.

Another big contributor to "abuse-like" appearances are dogs that have missed exposure and experiences during crucial early periods in their lives. This is often referred to as socialization. Dogs have critical periods when they're young—windows of opportunity—that if not taken advantage of and used appropriately, will often cause a myriad of behavioral fallout. Like the genetically compromised dog, these under-exposed, under-socialized dogs will often appear nervous, skittish, worried, jumpy, freaked out, and overly-reactive to their world. Many everyday objects (including people) will terrify them. This causes many people to create elaborate stories about abuse due to specific reactions to specific items. Something like "They were abused by a man who wore a baseball hat and black shoes," when in reality, they just didn't see this stuff early in their lives.

The third piece to the abuse puzzle is really more about exacerbating the above issues rather than being a creator of them on its own.

This is the leadership component.

In this context, I'm using leadership to mean training, exposure, working through issues, rather than avoiding them. A lack of leadership can take smaller genetic or socialization issues, and turn them into huge problems. And it can take bigger issues and make them monumental. Instead of a dog getting confident help and guidance about how to overcome (or improve) and deal with things they're concerned about, they instead get coddled and soothed and babied. Their fears are reinforced through their human's behavior, so the issues intensify. They're never pushed out of their comfort zones or challenged, so their world stays small and often gets smaller and smaller.

Once again, there are abused dogs. I've seen them. But the reality is, the vast majority of problem behaviors, fear issues, and other stuff that gets labeled as having an origin in abuse isn't abuse at all. It's far more often about what didn't happen to the dog, rather than what did. Genetics that didn't happen. Exposure that didn't happen. Leadership that didn't happen.

It's a great reality check, to remind people that while abuse does exist, it's far less prevalent than presented, and far less of a cause of behavior issues then most think. And understanding this is crucial to helping owners move from a place of feeling sorry for or making excuses for their dogs, to instead training, leading, and guiding them with strength and resolve.

And that's the only way to truly help your dog move forward, regardless of the cause.

when abuse DID happen.

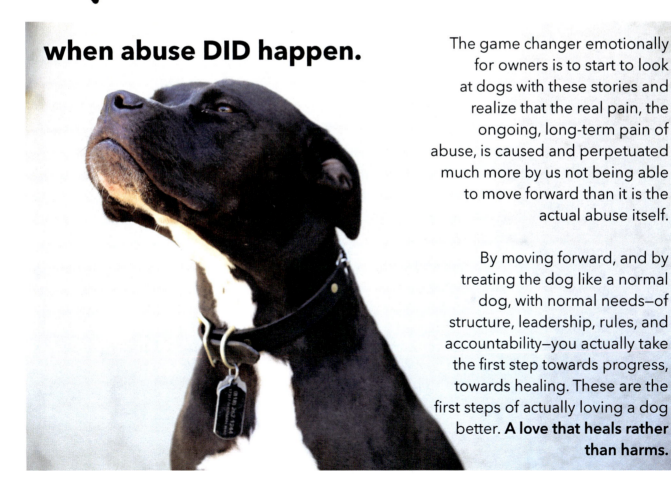

The game changer emotionally for owners is to start to look at dogs with these stories and realize that the real pain, the ongoing, long-term pain of abuse, is caused and perpetuated much more by us not being able to move forward than it is the actual abuse itself.

By moving forward, and by treating the dog like a normal dog, with normal needs—of structure, leadership, rules, and accountability—you actually take the first step towards progress, towards healing. These are the first steps of actually loving a dog better. **A love that heals rather than harms.**

HONOR YOUR DOG

Not every dog likes, feels comfortable, or enjoys the company of unfamiliar dogs.

And not every dog likes, feels comfortable, or enjoys the company of unfamiliar people.

Simple!

It's easy for us to have expectations and beliefs about how our dogs should be, what they should be capable of, and what should make them happy. But when we don't honestly take into consideration and honor our dogs' individual personalities, demeanors, limitations, and preferences, we do them a massive disservice. And we put them at risk for possibly getting into serious trouble.

The dog who is uncomfortable and insecure with other dogs, having to endure another day at the dog park—and often getting into scraps or all-out fights because of it. The dog who is uncomfortable and unsure around people, having to be "social" when guests are over—being tense, growling, snapping, or worse. The dog on a walk who is shy and insecure, having people come up excitedly to pet and engage, while his eyes are wide with fear and his body is tense and ready for fight or flight.

Our job as our dog's leader and guardian is to protect and advocate for them. To understand and prioritize what's best for them, rather than just what we'd like to see and believe. We need to be honest with ourselves about our individual dog, what his limitations are, and what helps or harms.

There's no shame in saying my dog doesn't like other dogs, or that he's not safe playing with dogs he's unfamiliar with. There's no shame in putting your dog away in his crate when you have guests over if your dog is terribly uncomfortable in that situation. There's no shame in saying no to folks who want to pet your dog on walks if your dog doesn't enjoy it or is uncomfortable with the interaction. In fact, there's not only no shame in any of the above, but putting your dog's comfort and safety first (as well as protecting other people and dogs) is your primary job and responsibility.

Don't let others pressure you to compromise your responsibility or let them question your decisions. If you know your dog and you know what's best for him, then do it, and don't let others influence you.

Of course, we want to always be improving our dogs and their ability to cope with their world and to thrive in it, but we also need to temper that desire with reality. Even as we're pushing for the very best from our dogs, we need to be sure we're being realistic and fair.

Don't put him in situations that overly pressure him, that make him terribly uncomfortable, and possibly put him at risk for making a bad choice. Tune into your dog and be honest. Work hard to understand his limitations, and then honor them. Give you and your dog permission to always do what's best for you both, regardless of social pressure or mythological expectations of what dogs SHOULD like and SHOULD be able to do.

Your dog is an individual. Treat him that way.

Don't ever let anyone make you feel bad about your approach, tools, or training method.

It's your life, **it's your dog.**

the drug that is **YOU**

How do you become a drug?

How do you go from being a healthy interaction to an addiction? How do you slowly unhinge your dog...through love?

When we lavish our dogs with constant praise, petting, attention, and the ability to be close (or actually on our lap) constantly, we're often setting the stage for addiction.

Our dogs, not knowing any better, simply gravitate towards what feels best in the moment. They get used to the consistency and intensity of emotional and physical interaction. This constant over-connection becomes a drug for them. They get used to it being ever-present, and like anything experienced consistently, it becomes something expected and depended upon. And then when it's removed, it's withdrawals time.

Without intending to, you've become a drug for your dog.

When you're not present, the gap or contrast is tremendous. Your dog feels emotional and physical distress—withdrawals—just like an addict.

This is typically seen as separation anxiety. Dogs that become frantic at departures. They often incessantly bark, whine, self-mutilate, destroy objects, and usually leave their biggest mark at exit points.

Much of the intensity of the reaction depends on the individual dog. Some are far more susceptible than others. But most dogs, given this setup over time, will develop withdrawal symptoms.

Because our dogs will accept whatever we share, the onus falls on us to make decisions and take actions that keep our dogs safe and stable. As much as it's your responsibility to ensure your dog doesn't run into the street, eat something toxic, or sit in a hot car, it's also your responsibility to keep them emotionally and physically safe...from you. Too much love, too much affection, too much access to your personal space, and too few offsetting rules and leadership are the perfect recipe to create an addicted, unhappy dog.

> If your dog is your whole world, you're going to have issues.
>
> You can't have a balanced relationship when you don't have a balanced life.

We've all heard the saying "It's not what you say, it's how you say it." How we say things conveys our true intent much more than the actual words themselves.

So many owners struggle with delivering commands in a tone, and with intent, that truly conveys what they want in a believable fashion. They want their dog to come to them, to sit, to down, to place, to heel, to leave it, etc.

But instead of delivering these commands believably, in a way their dog will actually listen to and honor, they ask, inquire, plead, or just half-ass the intent.

but do you really MEAN IT?

For many owners, I think they're afraid of hurting their dog's feelings or being "mean," or having their dog not like them. Demanding something from our best friends, and emotional support systems can be daunting for many. Owners feel uncomfortable and guilty and, well, just bad.

But presenting yourself in this soft, unsure, uncommitted, weak, boundary-challenged emotional space makes your dog uncomfortable. It makes your dog feel as if they're the most powerful (and stable) presence in their universe. And imagine how scary or empowering (depending on your dog) that might be. Dogs that have no one to truly lean on—in the positive, powerful, healthy sense—are typically very messy dogs.

They're dogs that are nervous, stressed, pushy, obstinate, anxious, fearful, ill-behaved, aggressive, etc.

Your voice betrays your true emotional state. It conveys who and what you truly are, as well as how you truly feel.

Are you too dependent on your dog? You can bet that demanding compliance will be tough. Is your dog your "soul mate"? You can bet setting rules won't be easy. Is your dog your "safe place" in the world? You can bet you'll struggle with holding him or her accountable. Is your dog a surrogate lover, child, or family member? You can bet you'll feel awfully guilty making your dog do anything that displeases them or make them look/feel unhappy.

Next time you're interacting with your dog, check your tone. Are you asking, inquiring, begging, or pleading? It might just give you some valuable feedback about where your relationship is, and where you're at emotionally.

Remember, sharing discipline, firmness, rules, expectations, and consequences doesn't make you a "bad" dog owner, or unloving. They actually make you the exact opposite.

LEADING vs. **leaning**

Is your dog there to keep you stable or do you keep your dog stable?

Is your dog your only emotional safe place, or are you his or her emotional safe place?

Does your dog view you as a powerful, healthy presence, or are you soft and needy?

Is good behavior demanded and expected, or is pushy, bratty, nasty stuff celebrated or allowed?

Do you spoil your dog because it feels good for you, even though it's making your dog a mess?

Do you provide the structure, rules, and discipline your dog actually needs to be happy, relaxed, and stable even though it's hard work?

Leading is hard. Leaning is easy.

One takes care of you. The other takes care of your dog.

What causes most aggression issues?

It's almost always a case of what we share and what we don't share with our dogs. Of course, genetics or severe abuse can cause aggression as well, but they probably amount to 1% of the cases we see. So that means that the vast majority of aggression issues are created...by us.

So what typically creates aggression?

- Too much permissiveness and allowing unwanted behavior

- Too much unearned affection, doting, and babying

- Too much freedom, access to all places, and access to personal space

the AGGRESSION recipe

- Too few rules, too little accountability, and a lack of valuable consequences for poor choices

- Unstructured, loosey-goosey, leadership-free environments

- Allowing a dog to be amped up continuously

- Reinforcing or rewarding behaviors that encourage bratty, pushy, possessive, protective, disrespectful attitudes and behavior

What fixes aggression?

- Examining all of the above, studying all the above, becoming aware of when the above are in play, and then working hard and consistently to reverse all of the above.

P.S. All dogs are different. Some dogs you can get away with much more of this stuff, and some far less. These are simply the causes we see most frequently creating the right dynamics for aggression issues. 🐾

When training your dog, it's easy to get caught up in focusing only on the obedience commands and how well your dog does or doesn't perform them. Training, and your dog, gets put into this small, simplified box.

But your dog's attitude, demeanor, and personality is far more complex and nuanced, and can't be summed up simply by a standard of how well they perform a series of rehearsed commands.

You can have a highly trained dog, a dog who knows all the commands and performs them fantastically but is still a disrespectful, pushy, brat. And at the far end of this you can have a highly trained dog that is seriously human or dog aggressive.

This is the stuff that is often missed. This is why many dogs are "trained" but still have issues.

It's not that the commands aren't helpful for creating a more respectful and safer dog; they are, but there are an awful lot of moments and behaviors that don't get covered in just obedience work. Developing the skill to look deeper, to feel more of what's coming back at you, not just the performance of commands, but the attitude in those commands and all the other moments, is where you'll find deeper, more helpful answers.

Snappy obedience can look great, but it can often be misleading, leaving us thinking that obedience equals a "good" dog. In truth, all it means is that your dog does a handful of behaviors well. It doesn't mean your dog is polite, respectful, patient, relaxed, or safe.

obedience vs. state of mind

Sometimes, the only thing standing between an ongoing issue with your dog—reactivity, barking, pulling, charging the door, jumping, counter surfing—is simply a firm consequence. You know, the stuff that makes poor choices uncomfortable, and good choices comfortable.

Because we've been conditioned to view any physical consequence as damaging to our dog, and our relationship, we've often been held hostage by our dog's bad behavior…and so have they. They live in a vacuum with no real feedback. So all parties suffer.

Could changing these frustrating and often dangerous behaviors be so simple? Sometimes, oftentimes, yes.

This word has taken on one heck of a beating.

For years we've associated punishment with abuse or harsh treatment. If you punish your dog or child, you've been taught that it's abusive and detrimental. It's stuff bad people do.

Let's see if we can't help rescue this term from the damnation it's unfairly received.

In behavioral terminology, **punishment is something that reduces or eliminates a behavior.**

That's it.

That doesn't sound so bad, does it?

There's nothing about abuse or harm. Reducing an unwanted, unhealthy behavior actually sounds pretty good...for you and the one doing it.

But we've still got this...*feeling* about it. We've been conditioned for years that punishment is bad, unenlightened, "old school." Instead, we've been taught a more evolved and humane approach: ignore the bad and reward the good.

But all organisms learn by what works AND what doesn't. What's comfortable AND what isn't. We can try to pretty it up, to seem more enlightened and evolved, but you can't escape reality. You can't escape how it all works...how we ALL work. You can't just say "Sorry, I only want to teach by what's good." (Well you can, and many do, but you won't get very far.)

Let's break this down. If you get pulled over for speeding and issued a ticket, and if it reduces your speeding tendencies, you've just been punished. If your dog is pulling on the leash and receives a quick correction, and if your dog slows down, he's just been punished. These are punishments administered.

If you've ever touched a hot stove, and you don't touch hot stoves anymore, you've just been effectively punished. If your dog runs into the sliding glass door, and decides to not to do that again, he's been effectively punished. These are punishments naturally occurring.

The goal of healthy punishment isn't to abuse, terrorize, or harm. The goal is to teach. To teach how to better and more safely navigate the world. Whether that be through nature or a human administering it.

And without punishment, you can't stop or lessen behaviors. It's right there in the definition. All you can do is reinforce other behaviors...in an attempt to avoid the ever-awful punishment. That's why so many dogs and owners are stuck. They've been taught to avoid punishment (often referred to as correcting) at all costs. It's unhealthy and damaging. But the truth is, NOT punishing, NOT giving adequate information about what is and isn't wanted, is actually the real cruelty.

Leaving dogs and owners stuck to struggle because they've been taught to leave out the one thing that can actually help them is a tragedy. The omission of punishment is the biggest cause of behavior issues, returned dogs, dogs being locked away in rooms or yards, and in many cases, euthanized.

We've all been hoodwinked for long enough. Do some research, dig deeper. Go beyond the commonly accepted wisdom of the day, and you'll find the one thing missing from helping your dog is likely the one thing you've actually known all along:

Discomfort changes behavior, often far more effectively than comfort.

I have always had dogs and felt fairly comfortable with how to train and care for them. In the first 6 months after adopting Frankie, a horrible event took place, out of ignorance on my part and just plain stupidity of a family member.

I had left Frankie alone with my 2-year-old nephew and my brother for about 30 minutes as I was out running errands. When I came home, I walked into chaos and my sister holding my nephew as he wails. I learned that my dog had growled at my nephew as he was trying to play and pull on her as she was under a chair. My brother did nothing about the growling except tell my dog to shut up. This escalated quickly and Frankie snipped my nephew in the face. If that was not bad enough, my brother threw my dog outside on a cement patio and punched her repetitively and hit her with a piece of 2x4. This was devastating and heartbreaking; I honestly did not know what to do. Some of my family members wanted me to put her down immediately, but of course, I refused to do so. At this point I realized Frankie was definitely going to be traumatized, as was I. This incident was tearing my family apart, and everyone was blaming everyone. I felt so overwhelmingly responsible for what happened to Frankie all I wanted to do was make it better. I was fearfully training my dog and secluding her out of fear of what could happen now that WE were traumatized.

After this incident I was terrified and a ball of anxiety and stress.

I was so afraid that she would hurt somebody else, as she was super reactive and started snapping and growling at almost everyone, including me. I was becoming afraid of my own dog, and I believed I was at fault for making her so scared. **I became trapped, I safeguarded both her and me by managing every situation. I felt this was the best thing I could do.**

For three and a half years we lived this way. I was so worried that something would happen to either her or someone else, so I always made sure I had an extra room in whatever house I was renting. I could not go on vacation or out of town without bringing her with me as she would growl at, snap at or be so scared she would not leave her kennel. I was convinced my life would be dedicated to making her safe in the only way I knew how.

The most constant thought in my head was, "Am I going to have to kill my dog for something I contributed in?"

I was honestly at the very end of my rope; I had zero hope in this training with The Good Dog, but I figured I would give her one last try. Frankie was very reactive, possessive, had bitten twice and has had years of seclusion. In an actual do-or-die moment, a few new friends helped me make this decision to give it all I had for this sweet pup who has been my number one.

So I did!

FRANKIE

After the Board and Train, I met with Sean and Cambre to see all the work they had accomplished. Training me was definitely the hardest part, but man-oh-man, Frankie has come so far.

We are able to go on walks in highly populated human and dog areas. Were she used to would flip out and bark and growl and try to get off her leash to lunge at dogs, she now walks right by my side, head forward and ears back—very calm! I can have friends over in my house without a constantly-growling Frankie. She can even be out in the house with people over, this was definitely never a possibility before. She is very well-behaved and calm, but also silly and playful without getting worked up into a frenzy. When I dropped Frankie off with TGD and gave them the story of what happened to her, I could not hold back tears from the guilt I felt for what happened to her. Sean said to me that I had to let go of this trauma and that is what would make the difference. So I made it my point to let go of it, and pictured that when I went to my first go-home session, I would be looking at a new, transformed Frankie.

That is exactly what happened.

I brought Franks and Beans home with me and really kept to the training.

I will tell you I have the best-behaved, happy dog I know! Thank you guys for truly changing our lives!

IT'S ALREADY **NEGATIVE.**

The negative association is already negative!

That's why you're seeing it.

If it wasn't negative, everything would be peachy.

Stop worrying about creating negative fallout by correcting your dog around things he's struggling with. He's already struggling.

Start helping your dog by **blocking the struggle.**

tellingSTORIES

One of the most damaging things we can do is to tell ourselves stories (or accept stories from others) about our dog's past.

There's no better recipe for messing up our dogs than to have a sad story constantly playing in our heads. These stories are the perfect emotional mechanism to prevent us from sharing discipline, structure, rules, leadership, and the other components of a healthy life together.

Tell these stories long enough and often enough and they BECOME who your dog is, and subsequently how you interact with him or her.

The stories become real...even if they're not.

Leave the stories behind. Train the dog in front of you. Live with the dog in front of you. Your dog needs a healthy future much more than it does sympathy for it's past. A past that may or may not be true.

"You can have an awesomely trained dog, that still misbehaves **if your relationship is broken.**"

babying your **TEENAGER**

You wouldn't think of treating your 15 year-old teen the same as you would your 2-month-old infant.

Babies and teens have totally different needs. Babies shouldn't have rules, accountability and all that; it's love, nurture, cuddle, feed...whatever you need, that's what you get. It's baby time! But imagine what you'd get if you treated your teen like a baby.

With all that allowing, enabling, and coddling you'd be on track to get a bratty, spoiled, entitled teen. When everything is given to you, you quickly begin to expect and demand it. But that's just the obvious stuff. You'd also get an insecure, unsure, dependent, and nervous teen. Because if you've never had to learn to do life on your own—to prove to yourself that you can handle problems and stress and find your own way—you'd never develop the confidence and resilience that comes from that struggle.

You'd have a bratty, entitled teen that would resent you for disabling them, for not giving them the tools they need to thrive.

And it's eerily similar with our dogs.

Baby your dog and watch the negative stuff come flying out. Watch the insecurity snowball. Watch them actually disrespect and resent you.

Confusing love with allowing and permissiveness sets you up to get the very worst from your dog or your child.

Be as believable in your **discipline**

The problem comes when we are out of balance.

It's not the affection or the freedom or the access on its own that is the undoing of most dogs; it's the absence of believable rules, structure, and accountability. It's the absence of the other side of the coin. The counterweight needed to keep things in check.

When we're as believable in our discipline as we are in our affection, we actually get to have more freedom, more fun, and more affection without creating negative fallout. And when necessary, we move seamlessly between the world of affectionate buddy and rule-enforcing leader in a heartbeat. And with no regret or guilt.

This is the simple formula that so many miss. They do the fun, easy stuff really, really well, but they do the hard, not-so-fun stuff...not so well. When they go to share rules or accountability, they do so with a lack of conviction and believability, and that's when things go sideways.

A good check-in is to ask yourself: am I truly as believable in my discipline as I am my affection? Do I cuddle better than I set rules? Do I play better than I share consequences? Balance these two worlds out, and you'll be on your way to a great relationship.

great EXPECTATIONS

Before you can ask for something, before you can demand something, and long before you can correct for something, you first have to teach it.

Fairly.

Dogs don't intuitively know what we want. They don't come to us knowing commands. They aren't pre-programmed, and they certainly aren't mind-readers.

But they are creatures of pattern. They tend to need lots and lots of patterning for a behavior to be 100% solid. Usually far more than we think.

So many owners have expectations of behavior...that they've never fairly taught. They might have shown their dog something, connected a word to it, rewarded the dog, and assumed it's all set.

But owners almost always miss the proofing process.

They think because a dog knows something in one context—usually a low distraction, calm environment—that the dog can or will perform the same behavior in a distracting, busy, or just different environment.

Dogs are super contextual. Change one thing in a sequence or cue or environment and your dog can be baffled.

Owners usually assume it's stubbornness or an attitude issue, but if you haven't proofed the behavior—with lots of distance, duration, distraction, and change of environment—your dog is probably confused.

Your gig? Teach *the entire process* before having expectations of awesomeness. Teach it slowly, teach it thoroughly, and teach it all the way to the end. Fully proofed.

Then demand greatness. :)

dismantling **DOGS**

The surest way to create dysfunction in our dogs is to ask them to fill an emotional space that should be filled by other humans. Whether it's the child you want to pamper and nurture, the romantic connection you long for, or the friend or family you desperately need, projecting all these emotions and responsibilities onto our dogs undermines our ability to have a healthy relationship with them. It creates unfair pressure, stress, anxiety, and dysfunction. It's our job to fulfill ourselves, not our dog's. Once we understand that clearly, we're set to build something healthy...and wonderful. If you want to get your dog right, you first have to get *you* right.

everything matters

When it comes to our dogs every conversation has value, every interaction means something, every rule enforced or not enforced is teaching...something.

Be aware that you are always teaching. Every moment is an opportunity to teach that you matter, that you have value as a leader and influence, or that you don't.

If we let 90% of the moments teach that we don't matter, we can't be upset when our dogs don't listen or respond in the 10% that we really care about.

Build your relationship in the easy moments so it's there when you need it in the hard ones.

go after the fuse, not the explosion

One of the most essential skills to help you sort out your dog's reactivity issues is timing! And the biggest mistake most folks make when working on their dog's reactivity issues is waiting too long to address the moment. Think of your dog's reactivity as a fuse. The longer you let it go the closer you get to the explosion point. But if you address the reactivity at the very moment the fuse is lit, you can usually avoid the explosion all together!

the PRESSURE COOKER

One of the most misunderstood aspects when working on reactivity issues on walks is...

Space.

And how it creates or relieves pressure.

If there's a crazy person loose in the state next to you, you're probably not very worried. If he's in your city, you're definitely more concerned, but not likely freaking out. If he's in your neighborhood you're going to be freaking out and barricading yourself in your home. If he was outside your door, well, it's real panic time.

That's the magic of space.

Get enough of it and just about anything scary or overwhelming is tolerable. Get too close to something unnerving and panic sets in. Sometimes all you need is a foot or two to be cool; sometimes it's a lot more.

But there are other pieces of the pressure cooker puzzle. It's not just space; it's also observable exit routes (are you guys trapped against a wall or fence?), and the demeanor of the approaching trigger (is it calm or crazy?). These all play a major role in how much pressure your dog feels, and more importantly, how he responds.

Regardless of whether it's fear based or excitement based, your job is to be highly tuned in to all these factors and to navigate them as best you can to your dog's advantage. Take that extra few feet (or across the street) from that barking dog. Don't get caught pinned in with no safe exit routes (always have a way out) in case dog or the other dog explodes.

As you and your dog improve, you can start to close the distance and deal with more high-pressure situations. But until then, be careful, be cautious, be strategic. Use all the advantages you can to ensure your success.

Space and strategy are your friends!

In the dog world we hear this term a bunch. "I need to socialize my dog with dogs or people."

The goal is to make them better with one or both. But unfortunately, it gets a ton of dogs and owners into trouble.

socialization, socialization, **socialization**

Let's clarify a few things. Socialization, correctly used, is a term to describe early exposure for puppies and young dogs. It's the process of ensuring pups and young dogs see lots of stuff and have positive experiences with them. The goal is to create a stable adult dog, who's seen and interacted with lots of dogs, people, different surfaces, environments, and of course scary things like cars, bikes, skateboards, trucks etc. Pups have critical periods—periods where, if not exposed to things (correctly socialized), they can grow up to be fearful and insecure of much of the world. So socializing them properly is a big deal.

But socialization has become kind of a catch-all term. It still means exposure, but now, any time owners have a dog with issues towards other dogs or people, they instantly declare their dog needs to be socialized. And unfortunately, the understanding of how to create that exposure, and what's needed to make it successful, is usually missing.

Owners decide their dog-aggressive dog needs to go to the dog park, or day care, so she can get more "socialization." They allow other stressed-out dogs to come up to their stressed-out dogs on walks in the hopes that the dogs will make friends. They invite strangers to approach and pet their freaked out dogs or have their nervous, growly dog "socialize" with guests.

This inevitably turns into a mess. Scuffles or all-out fights at the dog park or day care. The same with the new "friends" on walks. And the possibility of someone having been bitten while helping the dog to feel more comfortable with people is pretty high.

And even if owners manage to avoid the worst case scenarios, what they've guaranteed is that their dogs have far less trust in them, and whatever else it was they were concerned about.

So things have gotten worse, not better.

This is the usual fallout of what many owners consider to be "socialization."

The real trick is to create a dog that is 100% awesome with you. Lead, guide, share rules, share accountability. Get your dog into the most awesome training and state of mind space. Once you establish this, then you can start to consider healthy interactions. Then you can slowly start to bring your dog closer to the things they're worried about. But those interactions should be highly supervised, highly structured, and carefully chosen.

That means no dog parks, day cares, on-leash meetings, or forced human interactions. 🐾

The possibility of consequences connected to our actions shifts behavior.

When authority is present, and when consequences are possible or likely, behavior and choices typically manifest in their best way. When authority isn't present, and when consequences are unlikely, behavior and choices tend to be very different. We're all opportunistic to some degree. So are our dogs. When authority and consequences are absent, we usually get dogs' and people's worst.

Luckily, the opposite is also true.

Consequences drive all behavior.

the WAITING GAME

The waiting game consists of you and your dog in a situation that you know typically triggers him. Rather than correcting your dog at the very first moment of escalation—that split second of wrinkled forehead, ears up, breathing change —you wait to see if he's actually going to explode…this time. And what happens? Kaboom! You miss your moment, your window of opportunity, and your dog launches into his bad stuff. Again.

Usually this waiting game mindset comes from not wanting to correct our dogs. We worry that it's hurting them or making them uncomfortable. But here's the truth: allowing your dog to repeatedly get into a frenzied, stressed, anxious, or worried state about whatever it is that triggers him is actually the most awful and unkind thing you can do.

Correcting effectively, blocking escalation, and returning your dog to a relaxed and comfortable state—even if that requires a split second of discomfort to get there—is the kindest and most responsible thing one can do with a reactive, intense, nervous, fearful, or unsure dog. I often call the E-collar button a relaxation button because time and again, I watch stressed and tense dogs relax and return to normal once the button is pushed at a level the dog cares about. From staring and posturing to soft eyes and relaxed body posture.

So if we can start to see the correction as help, as guidance, as blocking unhealthy patterns, and not as a punitive "bad dog" thing, we might just be able to change up the waiting game. If we can make this shift, and see that in every possible trigger situation—whether on walks, when guests come in, or with tension in multi-dog homes—we only have a brief moment to effectively react, help, guide, and derail the escalation train. But if we play the waiting game, we're guaranteed to miss our moment, and our dogs are guaranteed to continue to struggle.

This might sound overly simplistic, but when it comes to dealing with reactivity issues with your dog, there are two problems that we tend to see trip up owners the most: They're either too slow to correct, too low when they do correct, or both.

TOO **LOW**
TOO **SLOW**

Either way, your dog is escalating, and you're late to the party.

Here's the thing: When it comes to reactivity issues, you only have a tiny window of time to be effective. Miss this window, and it becomes nearly impossible to de-escalate your dog. Once this window closes, most corrections will only make things worse.

So timing is critical, but so are the levels you're using. If you're too low, your dog won't notice the correction, and will simply escalate. If you're too slow, your dog will get ahead of you in the escalation process and explode.

The real trick to cutting off the escalation/explosion at the pass is to correct at the very first second of escalation. When the ears go up, when the eyes lock on, when the forehead wrinkles, when the breathing changes, when the dog just starts to speed up. And then make sure that correction level is significant enough to override the escalation. It's that balance of great timing and the right level that creates the magic.

Remember, the correction levels that work for your dog will change constantly. Different dogs, closer proximity, different environments, will necessitate quick adjustments in your intensity choices. Don't get caught on the numbers or second guessing yourself with your leash. Just watch your dog. He's the only one who knows what the right levels are. When his state changes, you'll know you're in the right neighborhood.

Get the timing and intensity right, and you'll be ready to make some serious progress.

"Little stuff always leads to big stuff."

MAKE SURE YOUR PRAISE **HELPS**

Let's talk about praise.

Everyone has been taught that if you say "good boy," or you pet your dog after it completes a command that you're reinforcing the command. Meaning, you're going to get more of what you want. Meaning your dog gets clear information that he's done the right thing.

Sounds good, right?

But here's the problem: when dogs are learning, most are struggling with the new behavior. They're struggling to focus, struggling with impulse control, struggling to stay in a heel, struggling to stay in place or in down or sit, struggling to stay calm enough to be successful.

What people are missing is that when dogs are struggling to hang in there and just putting the pieces together, excited praise and affection makes success next to impossible. It's a gigantic distraction.

You say "good boy," and he breaks his down. You pet his head while he's heeling and he speeds up. It's actually a setup. A setup to cause your dog to fail. (We actually use praise and affection as one of our biggest distraction and proofing techniques.)

The trick is, to make sure your affection helps and doesn't harm. When the dog is struggling, don't add any extra challenge to things. Allow her to focus and remove added distractions (you!).

When the dog is confidently executing the work, you can then give reinforcement...*if it helps*. 🐾

Your dog won't "hate" you for correcting him, but he will disrespect you if you don't.

if you won't advocate, YOUR DOG WILL

So many dogs show up here with dog or human aggression issues. And while there can be a multitude of reasons for these problems, **one cause we see often is owners not advocating for their dogs.**

For the dog aggression cases, many of these dogs have been roughed up, bullied, or attacked at the dog park, day care, or on the walk. After traumatic incidents (the more sensitive the dog, the less intense the interaction needs to be to cause fallout), we see dogs become severely reactive on walks and often dangerous with other dogs off-leash.

For the human aggression cases, many of the dogs have been forced to deal with unwanted petting, uncomfortable interactions, and people forcing themselves on them. These dogs are often more sensitive and insecure. Kids and strangers easily overwhelm them. If these interactions continue, the dogs eventually become reactive (barking and growling) and may become dangerous (actually biting).

The upshot for either issue is that when dogs repeatedly incur what feel like dangerous or uncomfortable interactions (even if *you* feel they should enjoy them), they eventually look for ways to find comfort and safety.

They take matters into their own hands.

That means owners, if they want to keep their dogs and others safe, need to be conscientious and tuned-in. Not every dog is Lassie. Not every dog is that bulletproof dog...especially if they've had bad stuff go down.

This, of course, doesn't mean our dogs need to live in a plastic bubble where nothing ever affects them. But it does mean that owners need to be cognizant of the situations they place their dogs in. They need to be realistic and honest. They need to be sensitive to who their dog truly is, what they can comfortably handle, and what they actually enjoy.

It's our job to protect and advocate for our dogs. If we won't do the work, eventually **our dogs will.**

What's the secret to building trust?

My bet is that it's not what you think.

It seems that most owners and trainers have it backwards. They try to build trust by being soft, sweet, accommodating, friendly, allowing.

So much of the dog training world has pushed the message of dogs needing our softness first. That to build a bridge of trust with a dog that is in a bad space behavior wise, we need to make them feel safe through removing stress, removing expectations, removing rules, removing accountability.

The message is, all of the above will make the dog worse. If we ask more of the dog, before we have trust, the dog will only trust us less. The stress of expectations will create mistrust and move the entire process backwards.

Ummm, B.S.

After working with over a thousand dogs, I can tell you, from experience—not from some lab study or ideological standpoint—that trying to create trust before respect is 100% backwards. It's actually the best way to create mistrust, keep a dangerous dog dangerous, and leave struggling dogs struggling.

Why? Because trust isn't built on allowing. Trust isn't built on being a doormat. Trust isn't built on "anything goes as long as you're comfy." Trust isn't built in a vacuum of leadership. All of these simply leave a dog in the same place (or worse) than when you found them.

That's enabling, not helping.

Not to mention, that allowing stuff is exactly what got these dogs into the space they're in now.

How do you trust something that is weaker than you? How do you trust something that is so soft that it has no ability to help? No ability to guide. No ability to draw the better out. No ability to share enough strength to block bad habits and choices, and override heavily entrenched fears and neurosis.

You don't.

You can't be pulled out of quicksand with a twig. But you can be pulled out with a branch.

Only strength can help those who are stuck.

So what if instead of allowing and enabling we did the opposite? What if we demanded more?

What if we established rules and expectations right out of the gate? What if we stopped the negative, unhealthy, or dangerous behavior? How would that feel for the dog? How would it feel to FEEL the beginnings of a change? Scary? Maybe at first. Stressful? Maybe at first. But soon, wow, what a relief. Wow, I'm less afraid, I'm less nervous, I'm more confident, I'm actually able to cope.

Someone has actually forced me to face my demons. Someone has actually forced me to be braver than I thought I could be. Someone has actually forced me to grow, expand, and develop. Someone has demanded my best.

And if you were that dog, the one who arrived a mess, but who started to feel better, safer, and more capable, would it maybe create trust? Could that strength stuff that is supposedly so terrifying and crippling perhaps be the exact thing to help a dog break through?

Could respect create a gateway for trust?

You betcha. Of course, it goes against everything most of the messages are preaching. But seeing dog after dog after dog is truly believing.

The upshot is this, whether it's dogs, kids, or even adults in trouble; the way out isn't through enabling and allowing. The way out is through demanding the very best. The way out and the way in is created through an atmosphere of respect and expectations.

And at the end of the day, what is more trusted than that which has relieved our suffering, shown us the way, and helped us reconnect to our best selves.

the gateway to
TRUST

THE FEARFUL TYRANT

Can you be fearful and a tyrant?

Sure. History is full of 'em. And it's no different in the dog world.

So many owners get tripped up with their fearful or insecure dogs. These guys or gals show up in owner's lives a mess. They cower, they shake, they hide, they avoid people and other scary stuff. Their body language and wide eyes tell the story of a scared and sad dog in need of love and rescue.

Our human nurturing button gets pushed, and bam, we're off and running.

We spoil, we love, we dote, we coddle, we shelter, we pet, we coo, we hold...

All with the very best intentions. To heal these broken dogs.

But what we miss is some simple psychology. You don't heal broken dogs by nurturing their brokenness. You heal them by guiding them out of their darkness and into the light.

You heal them by demanding their best. You heal them by expanding their comfort zones. You heal them by challenging them. You heal them through a love that is nurturing in its strength, not its weakness.

Trust me; the dog already has plenty of that.

But what if we don't realize this? What if we don't know? What if we only share the soft stuff?

Typically, what you get is an accelerated and enhanced version of all the dog's issues. They become more fearful, more insecure, more needy, more worried...more broken.

But there's more, and here's where it gets interesting; these dogs not only become more fearful, they also realize they can create whatever rules best suit them. And like any insecure figure with power, that's a dangerous recipe.

Feeling the leadership vacuum—meaning, no one is actually in charge of their world but them (you know, that freaked out, overwhelmed, frightened dog)—they become more stressed, more anxious...and more opportunistic.

With no rules in place, and no one leading, they go to work to make their world feel as comfortable as possible...for them. They decide that spot on the couch is theirs. They decide no one should be near their owner. They decide to snap whenever touched. They decide that every visitor is a direct threat. They decide that that toy is off limits to all but them. They decide that whatever they don't like, or whatever makes them unhappy or uncomfortable, gets met with their teeth or their growling.

This is when we realize that all the soft, nurturing, well-intentioned stuff we've shared has actually not helped. Instead, it's created a monster.

Instead of leading and guiding these freaked out dogs, we've allowed them to figure things out on their own. Instead of setting rules for appropriate behavior, we've allowed them to make up their own. Instead of helping by showing the way; by being a presence of strength, certainty, and firmness, we've left a vacuum. Even though we've meant well, the truth is, we've set the stage for enhanced dysfunction, and dangerous behavior.

We've created the perfect environment for the fearful tyrant. **The dog who is both afraid and empowered. And as history—and our dogs—has shown us, that is indeed a toxic combination.**

The masses will encourage you to spoil and be permissive (because that's what they do!). They'll even celebrate your dog's bad behavior. Misery and bad dog owners DO love company! Break away from the herd. Blaze your own trail.

You and your dog can do better.

I adopted my 150 pound mastiff, Dozer, from a shelter, not knowing anything about his behavior or past life.

When I brought him home, I allowed him a lot of freedom, feeling as if I had to compensate for the poor quality of life he likely had before me. I soon discovered he was completely untrained, so I had a positive dog trainer coming over to help with his potty training and basic obedience.

Unfortunately, just a few months after getting him, he became aggressive toward humans and dogs, lunging and barking whenever we went on walks and whenever unfamiliar people came over to our home.

When he finally bit someone, the trainer suggested I rehome him or put him down. Knowing that I had to exhaust every possible option for my dog before rehoming him or putting him down, I searched for YouTube videos on rehabilitating aggressive dogs, which is how I was introduced to The Good Dog. I began to understand that I was not providing my dog with enough structure, nor was I holding him accountable for his bad behavior. I was also giving him lots of unearned affection. As a result, he had become a disrespectful, bratty, easily excitable, entitled guy who thought he could do whatever he wanted without any consequences, and was frequently testing his boundaries.

After becoming more familiar with balanced training methods, I began taking away liberties from my dog and tightening up the structure, but it was already too late.

He already saw me as a soft owner.

He had become aggressive with me whenever I did something he was opposed to. He growled at me the first time I used a prong collar on him. He bit me when I ordered him off the bed, when I trimmed his nails, and when I cleaned his ears. Each bite was worse than the last.

After he bit me so severely that I had to go to the hospital for stitches, I became afraid of my own dog. I did not know when he would attack or what would set him off. I knew I needed professional help, and that is when I contacted The Good Dog.

After a four-week board and train with The Good Dog, Dozer has shown dramatic improvement. He is deferential and calm and is no longer intensely reactive. And with all the homework and tips The Good Dog team had given me, I am much more confident in safely keeping my dog in my home. I have made changes in my approach to dog ownership that allow me to be the owner my dog requires. I feel much more at ease taking him out on walks and hikes, even in places that are heavily trafficked.

The Good Dog truly changed my life, my dog's life, and the dynamics of our relationship. I am forever grateful for their help and continued support! My only regret is not finding them sooner.

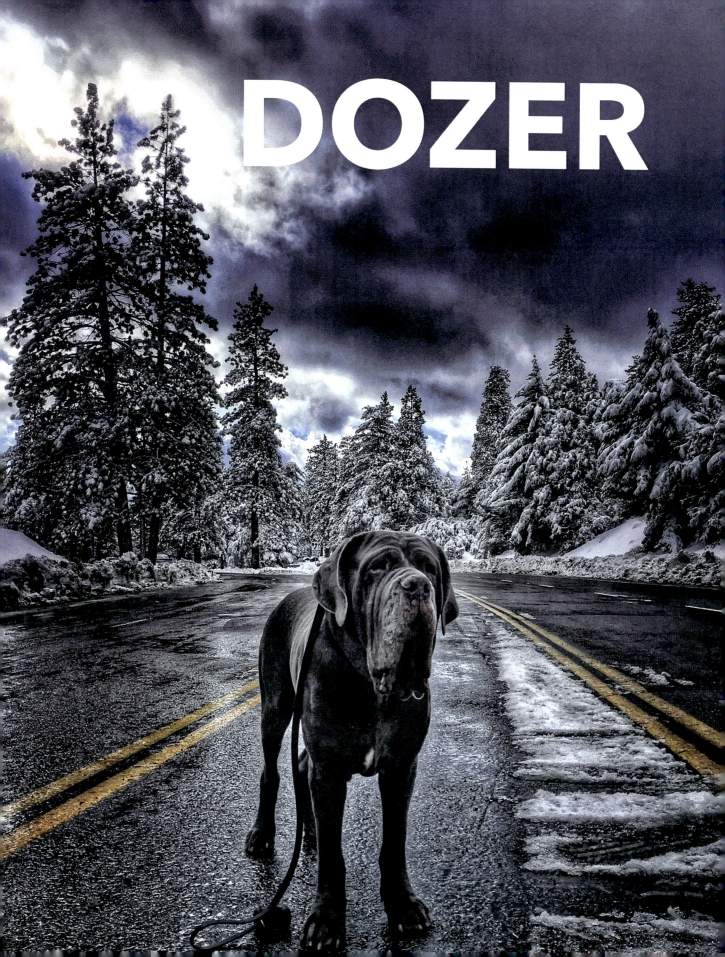

DOG TRAINING, THE GYM, DIETS, and SAVING MONEY

What do all of these have in common?

They all take consistent work and focus. None of them magically improve on their own, and all of them will fall apart if you lose your focus and get lazy.

It's human nature to go all in on something when we're excited, motivated, and the novelty is kicking! And it's also human nature to start to lose focus, momentum, and abandon effort as the initial excitement wanes. That's why people that excel at any of the above do so by making these things a lifestyle. They find ways to incorporate these activities into daily practices. Stuff they do, no matter what.

Habits.

The trick to long-term success with dog training, fitness, health, finances, or anything else, is to find a way to make these priorities something you can fold into your daily routine. Like brushing your teeth or taking a shower, they need to become automatic. You have to find ways to make them daily practices, not events that are tied to something currently exciting or motivating.

Excitement and motivation always fade. Only habits last.

Get excited about long-term success and results, not short-term blasts of change. It's slower and won't be as explosive or immediate, but it will be something you'll benefit from for the rest of your life.

Find simple, sustainable habits for anything that's important to you. Do the little stuff—the stuff that might not look like much in the moment. Do it consistently and watch your long game results slowly move you in positive, amazing directions. 🐾

LEADERS PROTECT,
followers get protected

Dogs are supposed to be protective, right?

Well, territorial behavior is definitely one of the reasons we brought dogs into our world. They made for great early warning systems.

But, over the years (with the exception of breeds specially chosen for protective work) we've selected more and more for dogs to be pets rather than guardians.

Of course, the bark at the door or gate to alert us of someone's presence is a welcome addition when it's just that...an alert. But when dogs go off the deep end, and when every person that approaches the property or enters the house is a serious threat—and one that creates dangerous, meltdown-level reactions—things have gone sideways.

When we see dogs in this state, we almost always see a corresponding lack of leadership, structure, and rules. It's this vacuum that creates the opportunity for protective/possessive behavior to explode.

So what's the real story here? When dogs don't have leaders, a whole bunch of stuff goes down. They're more stressed. They're more anxious. They're more worried. They don't get proper feedback about what is and what isn't appropriate behavior. So you get a stressed out animal making a bunch of important decisions...without any human guidance. And that's bad news.

The upshot is this: leaders protect, and followers get protected. If your dog is in a hyper-protective state, there's an awfully good chance that your relationship is out of whack and that you're not providing all that your dog needs in the leadership department.

P.S. If you have a breed who's actually bred to protect, you have an even bigger responsibility to make sure there's 100% clarity about who's in charge, or things can quickly become dangerous.

Look deeper. Look at the attitude and intent of the dog, not just the surface level behavior. **That's where you'll find your answers.**

If you've followed our work at TGD, you've probably heard one, if not all, of these favorite sayings of ours for helping owners wrap their heads around strategies for reactivity issues on walks.

What they all have in common is beating your dog to the emotional punch. Getting your dog out of the sequence of escalation before it gets so hot that you've lost him.

Getting and mastering these concepts is usually the difference between an owner struggling with their dog's reactivity or succeeding.

What we see is owners waiting to see if their dog is actually going to react. And we get it. You want to be fair; you want to give your dog a chance to succeed. But if your dog is truly struggling with reactivity issues, that moment where you wait to see if the explosion is going to come this time or not, that teeny window of time where he's loading, that split second when your dog first perceives the other dog, is your only moment. That's your only chance to catch that escalation sequence and cut it off at the pass. Your only moment to put out that little spark before it becomes a roaring forest fire.

Hopefully, the following suggestion might just make all this easier for you. Ready? Here goes: your dog doesn't need to be looking at other dogs on the walk. Period. That's not the purpose of the walk. And even though you might believe otherwise, not looking at other dogs won't determine your dog's happiness or fulfillment...and it won't make him sad.

He doesn't need it, and if he's got reactivity issues, he's definitely not ready for it.

Instead, make it easy for you and him. Just teach your dog that the walk is about walking with you and that his new job is to ignore dogs. Yep, ignore them.

Ignoring is the first step towards accepting.

And we do that by correcting our reactive dogs when they attempt to load up with an eyeful of another dog. We correct at a level our dogs care about, and we do it the instant we perceive a state change in our dogs.

A state change looks like this: ears suddenly up, forehead wrinkled, body stiff, speeding up

Go after the fuse, not the explosion;

too low too slow;

suddenly, breathing changing. Those are the beginnings, those are the signs you want to get extremely familiar with, and you want to address them instantly.

Once you get to barking, lunging, or growling, you've missed your moment. The opportunity to catch that sequence and block it is likely long gone. Getting to the right correction level at the right moment is the whole game.

But so many folks are worried (or have been programmed) that correcting their dog around other dogs or triggers they're reactive to will only make it worse. That it will create negative associations.

News flash: the negative associations are already there! That's why you have the reactivity in the first place! But by blocking and stopping the reactivity, you actually create a gateway, the beginning of a new way of perceiving the trigger, without all the accompanying emotional and chemical upheaval. And that's where you begin to change reactivity.

Any habit or pattern that gets blocked consistently enough, with the right timing and value, will start to recede and lessen. And it's the same with reactivity.

If you make it easy for yourself, instead of trying to walk the high wire or assessing grey area moments, and just decide that your dog isn't allowed to look at dogs (until he knows how to without escalation), you'll gain the certainty and timing advantage you need to successfully block, and eventually change reactivity issues. Why? Because you won't be hesitating, pausing, assessing. You'll just have a simple mandate: no looking.

With tons of practice, repeated exposure, and lots of positive reactions being practiced, you'll be moving your dog towards not caring about other dogs, and not needing to freak out.

How do we help so many owners get their dogs over the reactivity hump? Just like this. And I've yet to see a dog become worse or more worried or reactive from this approach.

Remember, you get a teeny moment when you can affect your dog's reaction. Don't miss it trying to decide if it's time to correct or not. Just follow this blueprint and you'll be off and running. 🐾

cap don't chase...

BUILDING AN **ATHLETE**

One of the biggest messages out there in dog training is the one about a tired dog being a good dog.

The premise is, if you'll just find a way to tucker your dog out consistently, he'll be happy, well-behaved, and chill. Your job is to find out how to exercise him or her enough to create this magic.

We see SO many owners struggling with this. They've bought into this popular message, and so they're out there walking, running, or bike riding their crazy dogs for miles and miles in an attempt to find that magic. They're hoping if they just exercise them enough the reactivity will go away, the fence fighting will go away, the crazy indoor behavior will go away, the going after guests or the other dog in the house will go away.

But here's the rub: how would you, the human, go about becoming more athletic, having more stamina, more go-go juice, more energy? You know the answer. It's an easy one. You'd work out, consistently. Would you be tired post-workout? Sure. Of course. But after a little rest you'd be stronger, faster, and more resilient. And because exercise is addictive, because it releases pleasurable hormones, you'd be dying to go tomorrow.

It's the same for our dogs. We exercise them like crazy, teach them to just go, go, go, and then we wonder why they're movement, action, and adrenaline junkies. We turn them into super athletes who need that daily fix. But even with the fix, after they've rested for a bit, they're still crazy and ill-behaved.

Exercise is super valuable. It's essential for a healthy and happy dog. BUT, exercise on its own doesn't teach your dog anything. It doesn't teach your dog better manners on the walk, or how to behave in the house, or improve any of the other problem behaviors.

It just creates an athletic dog who still behaves badly, and has plenty of juice to do so.

So what's the answer? It's actually two things. First, dogs need to learn how to slow down, calm down, relax, and chill when we ask for it, not just when they're tired. But they need to be taught how. They need to be taught calming exercises like duration place and down. They need to have both the on-switch and the off-switch. Second, bad behavior needs to be addressed directly, through training (using the right tools and approach), rather than through exercise. Trying to out-exercise bad behavior is running a race you can never win.

When you teach your dog how to turn off on command, and when you connect valuable consequences for nasty behavior, you'll be building an awesome dog, **not just an athlete.**

THE ART OF NEUTRALITY

What's one of the hardest skills to master? Emotional neutrality.

Specifically, emotional neutrality when sharing consequences or corrections with our dog.

So many of us get frustrated, freaked-out, overwhelmed, and even panicked when our dogs do something they shouldn't.

Most of us have struggled with trying to improve our dog's behavior, but with inadequate tools or training guidance, we've ended up on the losing side over and over.

See these problems enough and you start to take them personally. You start to anticipate explosions. You start to live in a panic state. You start to get pissed off that it's happening... again.

So correcting with a relaxed, confident, easy, and certain state of mind can be awfully hard. But it's an essential skill to develop. It's the best way to deliver the information to your dog without any extra emotional baggage. Baggage that almost always escalates the dog, and you, and makes everything worse.

Like I mentioned above, the right tools and guidance go a long way towards helping to keep you relaxed and neutral. But even with all that on your side, keeping your cool can be an elusive and challenging thing. But it's worth the work. 🐾

the danger of FAMILIARITY

Familiarity can create the illusion of transformation.

A dog-aggressive dog can often be slowly acclimated to a new dog or dogs and be totally cool. A human-aggressive dog can slowly be acclimated to new people and be totally safe. But that doesn't mean that either of these dogs is now not dog-aggressive, or now not human-aggressive. It just means the dog has become comfortable with the new situation.

The same dog that could be trusted with familiar dogs could be turned loose in a yard with a very sweet dog and attack it. And the same dog that was living nicely with familiar people could have a new human walk into the house and attack him or her.

It's so important that people understand this dynamic in order to prevent dangerous and disastrous situations from occurring. They need to understand that just because a dog becomes familiar and safe in one context, doesn't necessarily mean that that generalizes (transfers) everywhere.

With good training, many of the mindset issues that created these problems in the first place can be resolved, or tremendously improved. But that in no way guarantees that that dog will be safe in all contexts. New situations present new possibilities of choices and actions.

The best approach is to always be vigilant and aware and to understand that a dog becoming comfortable with a specific dog, dogs, human, or humans, isn't necessarily all better. He or she MAY be all better, but moving slowly and always understanding the possible dangers with novel situations is the key to future safety.

Dogs always do what works.

Make sure what works for your dog also works for **you**.

The Ten Commandments Of Dog Training And Ownership (Don't!)

1) Thou shalt not pet, soothe or share soft energy with a nervous, fearful, anxious, or aggressive dog.

What you pet is what you get. Only reinforce what you want more of.

2) Thou shalt not let your on-leash dog meet or interact with other dogs on-leash.

The stress, frustration, and worry of being trapped on-leash typically brings out the worst in dogs.

3) Thou shalt not let your dog pull you through thresholds, pull you on-leash, or pull you to sniff or pee.

These conversations, while seemingly benign, teach your dog to be pushy and ignore you.

4) Thou shalt not let two dogs that are new to each other "work out" their relationship on their own.

An old school approach to dog relationships that often ends in disaster.

5) Thou shalt not utilize the dog park without understanding the risks involved.

Many dogs are traumatized and taught not to trust other dogs, or allowed to bully and practice dangerous behavior here.

6) Thou shalt not use verbal or emotional intensity to control or correct your dog's unwanted behavior.

Adding these components, because they create stress, makes it much harder for your dog to process, comply and succeed.

7) Thou shalt not pick a dog whose physical energy is higher or whose state of mind is stronger than yours.

A dog whose physical needs and attitude displacement are stronger than yours will create relationship friction.

8) Thou shalt not let your off-leash dog run up on dogs walking on-leash.

Because one dog is free and the other is "trapped" this is the perfect way to create dog fights, reactivity, and frighten dogs and owners.

9) Thou shalt not baby, spoil, or humanize your dog.

Sharing only soft stuff with your dog causes them to feel unsafe, entitled, and insecure.

10) Thou shalt not mistake anxiety or excitement for happiness or calm relaxation for sadness.

Fast motion and activity do not equal a happy dog. Just like stillness and holding a command doesn't equal a sad dog.

The Ten Commandments Of Dog Training And Ownership (Do!)

1) Thou shall only pet, soothe, and share soft energy with a dog when they are in a healthy and positive state of mind.

If you reinforce the mental state you want, you'll get more that state.

2) Thou shall keep your on-leash dog safe by not allowing interactions with unknown dogs who are also on-leash.

It's your job to advocate for and keep your dog safe by preventing unwanted interactions.

3) Thou shall ensure your dog waits patiently at thresholds, heels politely, and obeys the rules of the structured walk.

Ensuring that these "small" moments are politely observed guarantees better overall behavior, attitude, and relationship.

4) Thou shall always supervise and direct the interactions of dogs who are new to each other.

Directing interactions, advocating for, and insisting on polite behavior creates the best chance of a successful introduction.

5) Thou shall utilize the dog park at you and your dog's own risk.

The best way to avoid the negative fallout from dog parks is to avoid them.

6) Thou shall use a calm, relaxed tone and energy when interacting with and correcting your dog.

Avoid adding negative emotional baggage, which can lead to nervousness, and mistrust, to your communications with your dog.

7) Thou shall pick a dog whose physical energy and attitude is compatible with your own.

The best way to ensure a great relationship, and to avoid conflict, tension, and major problems, is to start off with a good physical and emotional fit.

8) Thou shall always have control of your off-leash dog and prevent it from harassing or attacking other dogs and owners.

It's your responsibility to ensure that you have complete control of your dog when off-leash. Off-leash dogs attacking on-leash dogs is one of the biggest causes of reactivity and aggression.

9) Thou shall honor your dog and keep her balanced and healthy by sharing rules, structure, accountability, and treating her like a dog.

The best way to create a stable and happy dog is to provide for their true needs, rather than what is simply easy or enjoyable for us.

10) Thou shall appreciate and cultivate your dog's ability to be quiet, still, and relaxed.

Teaching a dog how to "turn off" and simply relax is one of the greatest gifts we can give them. Appreciate it and savor the benefits.

part THREE
the solutions

it's a PROCESS

When you finally decide it's time, time to work on training and sorting out whatever behavior issues your dog (and you) may have, you gotta remember, it's a process.

I know that seems obvious, and maybe simplistic, but it's easy to lose sight of the fact that you and your dog have likely been doing this dance of dysfunction for a long time. It's easy to want the changes, to be putting in the work, and feel like it's not happening fast enough. So here are a few reminders...

You've both got habits that are likely deeply ingrained—they need time to be addressed and replaced.

You're both learning new skills and mechanics—they need time to develop and be mastered.

You both have emotional associations and triggers that cause you to feel a certain way in certain situations—they need time to be overhauled and worked through.

You're both learning new ways of thinking and feeling about each other—you both need time for this process to develop and crystallize.

You're both adjusting your daily lifestyle and routines of how you live together—you both need time to adjust and become comfortable.

Expect things to be bumpy, painful, challenging, annoying, and frustrating. At times you might feel hopeless. At others, victorious and amazing. Like all journeys, it'll be a combination of ups and downs. Expect it.

Change is hard for all of us. You, your family, your friends, and your dog...you're all learning a new way of being, of interacting. That's hard stuff!

So please remember to give you and your dog the time and space needed to undo all the old stuff and to start building all the new stuff...especially at the beginning, when things are at their hardest. If you go in expecting challenges and difficulties, you'll be ready for battle. The battle of change. And change is most definitely a process.

PERMISSION-BASED TRAINING

What if I could share with you one of the biggest secrets to successful training, and successfully turning crazy dogs into polite, cool customers?

And what if I told you this incredibly effective training approach was actually super simple?

You might not believe me. It might sound too good to be true, but I promise you, it's the real deal. It works, really well, and when you get the concept, it's actually pretty easy to implement and put into practice.

So what exactly is this training "miracle"? Well, it's not really a miracle at all. It's actually just a simple process of changing a dog's state of mind, attitude, and creating some awesome impulse control and respect.

We call it Permission-Based Training. And it really is as simple as it sounds.

By teaching dogs that they need to ask for permission before making decisions, especially the ones they're jazzed up about, we lay the foundation for some serious training magic.

It's a major psychological shift for the dog, and it almost instantly changes the human/dog dynamic to a more healthy, positive one.

What does the opposite of Permission-Based Training look like? Dogs that are on auto-pilot, with zero impulse control and no conscious thought for their choices or actions...basically, a "feel-do" mindset. Meaning, whatever the dog feels it wants to do, he simply does it, regardless of what might come of it. Practiced long enough, this auto-pilot mindset becomes default. Dogs simply have an impulse and they act on it.

They bolt out of crates, out of doors, out of cars. They jump on and push people around. They run away and refuse to come when called. They pull on-leash and blow up at other dogs. They're frenzied and frazzled. They basically live in their own world, with no regard for anyone or anything.

So how do we consistently turn all these challenging, nutty, bratty, aggressive dogs around? We jump into our PBT approach right out of the gate. And as soon as dogs realize that someone's in charge, that there are rules cooking, and that there's accountability for breaking those rules, we see some pretty massive changes...and fast.

We see dogs calm down. We see dogs start to actually think about their next choice. We see dogs behaving in a more polite and respectful fashion. We see dogs viewing humans as something relevant. We see that edgy, jacked-up, pushy dog slow down, chill out, and share an entirely different side of him or herself.

It's kind of amazing to watch.

The real trick is to know where to look for these moments, and be ready before they go down so you can get the drop on your dog. If you see them coming, you can be prepared to share just the right conversation, and start to create an awesomely behaved dog.

To help you with this, here are a few examples of common situations where excitement and intensity tend to take over. These are great opportunities for you to work on creating your own PBT:

• Crate (permission to go in or out)

• Thresholds (permission to go in or out)

• Place command (not leaving unless given permission)

• Eating (waiting for release)

• Peeing/sniffing on walks (waiting for release)

• Walking in a structured "heel" fashion (unless released)

• Any command that the dog has been asked to be in (must wait for release)

• Furniture (wait for permission)

• Personal space (wait for permission to access)

• Getting in or out of the car (wait for permission)

• A bomb-proof recall (must always come back on command, wait for permission to roam or not—perhaps one of the greatest impulse control exercises)

• And any other contexts where you see a lot of excitement, pushiness, intensity etc.

Teaching your dog to look to you, to ask permission before simply acting or reacting, is the true secret sauce to transforming both behavior and attitude. It also creates a more relaxed, respectful, thinking dog. And who doesn't want that?

"There's a difference between teaching your dog what you want him to do and what you don't want him to do. One is about saying yes (rewarding), the other is about saying no (correcting)."

"If you're not providing both, you're setting your dog up to fail."

THE SECRET TO **TRANSFORMATION**

Truth be told, we almost never address issues head on.

What we do is what we always do—**we work our foundational program.** And this is something I see so many owners and trainers miss.

They go after the symptoms, rather than the core issue. And the core issue is almost always a bigger state of mind problem.

When I first started out as a trainer, I used to address each problem head on. Resource guarding? Go after it. Crazy reactivity issues? Go after it. Growling at guests? Go after it.

This was the least leveraged, least comprehensive, and least effective approach. It was also the hardest on the dog, on me, and the owner.

Typically it meant going after big symptoms, in their biggest expression. Hard stuff. Stuff that needs way more pressure and higher correction levels to have any impact.

When I discovered the value of an overall state of mind approach, everything got easier...for all of us. And the results were far more profound and lasting. What we found was that most of the symptoms either disappeared or were far easier to address once the foundation was in place.

If there's one thing I'd love for you take from this book it's this concept: the value of a more comprehensive, foundational approach. Removing stress, anxiety, and overwhelm that arise due to a lack of structure, leadership, and accountability.

This doesn't mean there aren't times for a more direct approach to certain issues—there are—but if that's your primary strategy, you're doing things in the hardest, most dangerous, and least effective fashion, in a big-picture sense.

Prioritize the big picture, the foundational issues, and you'll see some amazing things happen.

the MAGIC formula

Address the smallest infraction or behavior shift, the split second it begins. And do so with enough intensity that it stops cold.

Too simple, too easy, right?

Nope.

Whether it's reacting on walks, growling at the door or a guest, running off to chase a dog, guarding a toy or food...

Most owners struggle with this. Whether it's the actual timing (not seeing or reacting to the beginnings of the escalation), or correcting/addressing too mildly (they see a small reaction and thus share a small consequence), this is almost always the stumbling block that prevents success.

These owners end up behind their dog's escalation. They end up "chasing" their dog's behavior, (with annoying and frustration-inducing corrections) and making it worse, rather than "capping" it (a well-timed correction with the right intensity) and cutting it off at the pass.

Mastering this concept, by becoming adept at seeing the FIRST sign of a behavioral shift, and getting your timing and reaction so solid, and so quick...and ensuring the intensity is just right...is a skill that all great dog trainers have in their toolbox.

You can have it too. It just takes practice, focus, and the clear understanding of the value of timing and intensity.

The beauty of this simple formula is if you consistently catch the problem at its smallest, lowest level of intensity, and do so effectively, you'll likely never see the problem in its full bloom.

Whether it's fear, anxiety, reactivity, dog aggression, human aggression, resource guarding, stubbornness, attitude issues - whatever - the question is, are you stronger than these issues? Are you more determined, more resolute, more patient, more creative, more assertive, more dedicated, and more resourceful than your dog's issues? If there's any secret to training and transformation success, especially with challenging stuff, these decisions are it.

are you STRONGER than your dog's WEAKNESS?

And regardless of what you're facing, the good news is, you can always improve it. You may not be able to make it perfect, but you can always make it better! It's always comes down to how bad do you want it, how hard are you willing to work, and how much are you willing to change? #DeterminationRevealsAnswers

"PULLING" DOGS

Can you "pull" a dog in your direction? Can you change a dog's emotional state through what you share with him or her?

You betcha.

If you know how to harness your speech, your body language, your breathing...your entire presentation...you can absolutely "pull" a dog in the emotional and physiological direction you desire.

This doesn't mean you're all-powerful and have cosmic abilities to instantly transform who a dog is or how they're feeling. But it does mean if you're aware and understand and practice, you can absolutely have a profound effect on a dog's reactions.

Want a nervous, insecure, anxious, reactive, or even aggressive dog to calm down, relax, focus, trust you, make better decisions, and be safer?

Become highly conscious of your entire conversation.

Slow your breathing. Slow your body movements. Ensure all your body motions are fluid and non-angular or jagged. Quiet your voice and slow your speech. Quiet your mind too.

Do all this confidently—not mousy, not scared, not nervously, not sweetly; just calm and neutral and relaxed. You'll find you're able to "pull" dogs into a different state. A state where you can actually help them move forward and follow you to a better space.

P.S. Do the opposite: move fast, speak fast, breathe fast, move jaggedly, and you and the dog are guaranteed to have a tremendously hard time.

why HEEL matters

So what's the big deal about the whole "heel" position thing anyways? Why do trainers want dogs to walk like this? What's the value behind it?

Good questions.

First off, we don't do anything just for looks. Our training approach is all results and practicality based. So we don't do heel for tradition or aesthetics. (Even though a heeling dog DOES look good!) So then why this whole heel thing? Because we've found that the majority of issues that owners struggle with on walks (barking, lunging, pulling, and generally freaking out) disappear once a dog is taught to heel properly.

Why is that?

Because heel is about much more than a position, it's about a mindset.

Let's take a look at how this all works.

•Dogs in heel are focused. Not on everything else in their world, but on you. Because they have to utilize a ton of impulse control, awareness, and focus on keeping themselves in position, dogs who are prioritizing this stuff aren't prioritizing the bad stuff.

•Dogs in heel are relaxed. Dogs doing the work of keeping themselves in heel, and not simply being held back by the owner or flailing around, aren't amped up mentally or physically. They're focused on their work, their position, their speed. And that self-focus creates more relaxation and less stress, concern, worry, and excitement about the environment.

•Dogs in heel are calm. Dogs walking with you, at your pace, being tuned-in, looking to you for guidance, and ignoring the craziness around them are calm dogs. Calm dogs don't freak out.

•Dogs in heel are working. Walking in heel is like you studying for a test. It's a ton of brain work. Not only does this work keep dogs focused on more healthy stuff, but it will also tire dogs out far more than a non-structured, crazy walk will.

•Dogs in heel are polite. The simple act of creating a structured position, one the dog has to maintain and one that has consequences for breaking that position, creates a polite, tuned-in, respectful state of mind.

•Dogs in heel can't cheat. The heel position is a great barometer of your dog's state of mind. If your dog gets distracted or starts to escalate due to another dog, you'll almost always speed up or slow down. This will tell you there's something cooking that you need to address.

- Dogs in heel are being led. Dogs in heel are being guided by their owners. They're deeply connected to you. If you actually lead the walk, you'll find your reactive dog is more confident about things he's unsure about and more polite about things he'd like to go crazy over. Because your presence, relationship, and demands brings out the best.

- Dogs in heel have better relationships with their owners. Dogs who honor your requests to walk a certain way, at a certain pace, with a certain demeanor, are dogs that have positive and respectful relationships with their owners.

- Dogs in heel are safe. Because they're close and calm, and looking to you for direction, they're far safer around things that could harm them as well as safer around things they could harm.

The reality is, dogs that are freaking out on the walk - pulling, lunging, barking - and being a menace to the neighborhood (and you), are dogs that are almost always missing all of the above.

the CUSHION

Okay, let's talk about the cushion.

What's the cushion?

The cushion is the thing that either works for you or against you...depending on how you use it. It's the space between your dog behaving and exploding. It's something you can control and navigate, or totally miss.

Let's think of your dog's behavior on a scale of zero to ten. At zero, we have a calm, chilled out dog...maybe asleep! At ten, we have a dog in full explosion mode. In between, we have our cushion. The amount of cushion you have will determine several things. First, it will determine how long you have to react. Second, it will determine how much pressure/correction you have to use. Third, it will determine if your dog is able to hold it together (with or without your help) and ride the wave of escalation without hitting the breaking point. And fourth, it will determine if you even have an opportunity to successfully address the behavior at all. (And there's actually a fifth point, too. It'll determine how comfortable or stressed out your dog's life is.)

A dog that resides at the high end of the scale (say a 7, 8, or 9, which is where most troubled dogs live), has very little wiggle room between where it's at and the big 10 of explosion. These are the dogs barking at everything that goes by the window, charging the front door and guests, exploding at every dog on walks. A dog that resides more in the middle (4, 5, 6) has more room. And a dog that resides at 1, 2, or 3, has lots more.

That's why it's imperative that we don't just try to address the moment of explosion. That's a losing proposition—and one so many owners get caught in. Once in the 8, 9, 10 area, your goose is cooked and so is your dog's.

To be successful we need as much cushion as possible.

Think of a reactive dog cruising around on a walk, all revved-up and on the precipice of trouble. He's bouncing around at 7, 8, or 9. Pulling, scanning for trouble, coming out of his skin. The mental space between 7, 8, or 9...and 10...is tiny! And boy, does that space close fast! Once this dog gets an eyeful of another dog, he's gonna hit that 10 in a heartbeat. KABOOM! You can try to correct, but it was too late before you even tried. Your dog is way ahead of you, mentally.

But, if you could get that same dog down to a 2, 3, 4, or even 5, you'd have a much better chance at success. You'd have so much more cushion. A calmer, less revved-up dog to work with. A dog that's still able to be positively influenced and directed.

How do you get more cushion?

An immaculate heel and structured walk with zero pulling. Threshold exercises at crate and front door. Duration work inside the house to teach calm. Consequences for inappropriate behavior. And that whole rules, structure, and leadership thing.

Practice all that as we prescribe, and we promise you'll get way more cushion to work with. And way more success.

P.S. Correcting dogs at the explosion point is typically when owners get bitten or redirected on by their dogs. At this point of escalation, corrections just add more fuel to the fire. Don't do them. 🐾

The one consistent theme I've seen with owners that have succeeded with challenging dogs: 100% determination to solve the problem...

and zero excuses.

3 THINGS YOUR REACTIVE DOG WANTS TO KNOW

These three go in the "simple, but not easy" category. I've narrowed them down in order to help owners better wrap their minds around how this stuff works...or doesn't.

Ready? Here we go:

1) Can you believably control yourself? In times of stress and pressure on walks or elsewhere, are you calm, relaxed, confident and in control? Or are you unsure, nervous, tentative, angry, and stressed?

2) Can you believably control your dog? In times of stress and pressure on walks and elsewhere, are you able to use tools, training, and strategies to keep your dog calm, relaxed, tuned-in, and respectful?

3) Can you believably control your environment? In times of stress and pressure on walks and elsewhere, are you able to protect your dog from unwanted human or canine intrusions?

Like I said, these are simple, but not easy. Mastering them will likely be an ongoing endeavor. But the more you chip away at the problem areas, the more you understand these dynamics, and the more you up your game with these three, the more you'll find your reactive dog...not reacting.

winning the BATTLE of dog-reactivity

Question: When do we win the battle of dog-reactivity?

Answer: Long before the fight.

Wanna know a gigantically important training secret? You don't overcome reactivity issues by searching out dogs and correcting your dog that is melting down around them. And you certainly don't overcome reactivity issues by stumbling into dogs with a loaded weapon...that you didn't even know was loading.

That's how you lose the battle.

What so many miss is that reactivity is a battle that you win (or lose) long before you see a dog or other trigger.

If you can see your dog as something that loads up and then explodes—like maybe a slingshot—you might get a better handle on the concept.

What escapes and undermines so many is this loading process. They think their dog is just "reactive," they don't realize they've allowed the slingshot (their dog) to load and load. They've set the table for the reactivity. They're allowed so much tension, before they've even seen a dog, that once that dog comes into view...pewwwww!

The dog that pulls on-leash is loading. The dog that zig-zags back and forth is loading. The dog that marks and sniffs wherever is loading. The dog that pulls out the front door like a rocket is loading. And the dog that is a mess in the house is loading.

All these small, seemingly insignificant (or disconnected) moments are the actual battle. The problem is, you didn't know the battle even started.

This is why we're always harping on about "state of mind" training. Because if the state of mind is right, everything else gets easy. Or at least, a lot easier.

State of mind is the actual battlefield. That's where you win or lose.

If you can see the big picture, and if you can prioritize overall state of mind rather than just addressing individual moments of "badness," you'll be set to have a fighting chance.

Here are a few tips to help you (and your dog) to win the reactivity battle:

BIG PICTURE

-See all moments as connected. Nothing lives in a vacuum with your dog. Pushy, bratty, amped-up behavior in one place is going to show up everywhere. From the house to the walk and vice versa.

-See how little "benign" moments load up into big moments. If we address the small ones, we rarely see the big ones. **(Re-read this one...often.)**

-Allowing your dog to ignore you anywhere is training your dog to ignore you. And guess where that ignoring will come out? Right where you don't want it.

-See how a lack of structure, rules, and guidance on the walk (and preceding it) lead to an amped-up, disrespectful dog. And an amped-up, disrespectful dog is a loaded dog.

-Understand that you don't get "buy-in" just when you need it. "Buy-in," or a healthy relationship dynamic (deferring, listening, respecting), is something you build and create long before you need it.

-Understand how dogs load (especially your particular dog) and also how you best diffuse that loading.

SPECIFIC PICTURE

-Dog waits patiently at threshold for your cue.

-Keep the leash short, but not tight.

-Start with a firmer conversation right off the bat to set the tone for the walk.

-Never use constant tension to hold your dog back. This creates massive loading. Use the prong or E-collar correctly to ensure the dog does the work, not your arm.

-If these corrections aren't working, do 180's. You can perform these with prong or E-collar.

-Never allow pulling to a bush, grass, or a tree. Release the dog on your word to sniff or potty.

-Think of your walk as a 90/10 proposition. 90% of the walk is a structured heel, 10% is sniffing, pottying, and freedom.

-Correct any small escalation the second you notice. Pulling out of heel, looking at another dog. Don't warn or nag. Correct in a valuable fashion.

-This is so important I'm going to say it again: don't wait to see if your dog is going to escalate or explode. That's how owners lose. He IS going to explode. Correct the instant your reactive dog looks at the other dog or speeds up. This will de-escalate your dog, and teach him to focus on the walk, not other dogs. **(Re-read this one...often!)**

-Use space as a buffer to help reduce the pressure and intensity your dog feels. The closer you are, the harder it is for your dog to hold it together, the higher your corrections will have to be, and the less time you'll have to correct.

-Focus on creating a polite, courteous, respectful dog at all times, and this will eventually become your dog's default.

The wise owner understands the loading process. He or she knows that everything and every moment counts. They focus on building an awesome state of mind long before encountering other dogs, and work hard to maintain that state of mind throughout the walk. 🐾

The right tool is the one that helps you and your dog to **succeed.**

natural counter-conditioning

Over and over we see and hear about owners who have been told that correcting their dogs around triggers (dogs, people, cars, vacuums, etc.) will only make things worse. That the correction will create a negative association.

So owners, of course, not wanting to make things worse, avoid correcting their dogs around triggers. And where exactly does that leave owners and dogs??

Stuck.

Stuck with the same behavior, except that it usually just gets worse and worse. The reactivity on walks gets more explosive. The reactions around guests at the house get worse. The reactions around the dogs at the fence get worse.

So what's an owner to do? If you believe the prevailing, popular dog training "science," you're screwed. You've got the perfect catch-22.

Correct and make it worse. Let it go and make it worse.

What if there was another choice? What if there was something that actually made things better? What if that something flew in the face of popular "science-y," training approaches?

While I'm not here to convert anyone, I am here to tell the truth as I've seen it. The truth of over a thousand dogs speaks awfully loud.

Let me see if I can explain how this REALLY works.

Here's the biggie. Are you ready for it? If your dog is reactive—on walks, in the house, in the yard—the negative association that everyone is trying to scare you about, is already in play. If your dog felt comfy around other dogs, people, or whatever the trigger might be, there wouldn't be a negative reaction.

Please read that last sentence again. It's not fancy or super complicated; it's just some simple cause and effect stuff.

If your dog felt good about these triggers, you'd get good reactions. Right? So if we can agree that the negative association is already in play, then we can let go of that catch-22 road block.

So the how does this work? And what's this "natural counter-conditioning" all about?

Here's the deal: Your dog sees the trigger, the emotional pattern of escalation and intensity begins. In split seconds stress, worry, anxiety, fear, overwhelm, and panic set in.

As the mind elevates and starts to take off, so does the body. Left unchecked, your dog is likely set to explode. Barking, lunging, growling, rearing up, spinning around, darting forward to bite or nip, etc.

But if at this first moment of escalation you intercept—if you correct firmly and early enough—you can actually cut this emotional escalation off at the pass. If you stop, block, or interrupt this reaction with a correction that is valuable, you stop the reactivity train at the station.

And here's the best part. If you consistently practice this corrective process - and you do so early and with enough intensity and enough space - you can start to build a new emotional pattern. You can actually reprogram your dog's reactions and feelings.

But wait a second. How the heck is correcting my dog around the things he's freaked out about going to help build positive associations? Very good question.

And here's the answer: If you block the negative reaction long enough, your dog begins to experience an emotionally neutral feeling around the triggers. And emotional neutrality is the first step towards moving towards a more positive emotional experience. A neutral feeling is a feeling that is open to experiencing and developing new associations and feelings.

They may not be positive at first. That's okay. First, let's get out of the negative feeling and reaction. Then we can move into the neutral feeling and reaction. And from there, with enough repetition, we can actually create a gateway for a positive feeling and reaction.

The only way to continue a negative feeling and reaction is to practice it. And the only way to create a neutral, and eventually more positive feeling and reaction is to practice it.

This is "natural counter-conditioning." Meaning, we're not using all sorts of extra reinforcers to create or manufacture the feelings. Instead, we're using the dog's natural emotional programming. That being, if the dog's not having a negative freak out, she actually has a chance to create new associations or feelings. Something has to fill the emotional void.

Once a dog learns that something isn't going to hurt them, and once you teach them that melting down and freaking out isn't an option, you might be surprised what they learn and the new feelings that develop.

Naturally.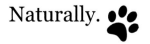

the ART OF CALMNESS

So why the focus on calm? What's the value? Aren't dogs supposed to be running around crazy, having fun?

Lots of good questions.

Let me say this first. If you have one of those cupcake dogs—you know, the ones who can go anywhere, meet anyone, and play with any dog without issue—then this isn't for you.

But, if you're one of those owners who have a less-than-perfect dog, or maybe a far-from-perfect dog, learning the value of calm and how to cultivate it can be a game changer.

So what's the value of it? If you've got a dog that is reactive on walks, reactive in the house, anxious, stressed, fearful, or obsessive, calmness can have a major impact.

Most of the dogs listed above struggle with arousal issues. Arousal being an amped up mental and physical state. The canine version of being stressed out and anxious. These dogs often seem frenzied, edgy, and barely hanging on. In this state, these dogs are highly agitated, uncomfortable, and overwhelmed by their very being. These dogs use constant motion and activity to obscure deeper issues.

Imagine you in your most harried space. Wildly late for a super important appointment...and stuck in unmoving traffic. (Or substitute any situation that would make you crazy.) We've all been there. And I'm sure if we're all honest, we'd all agree we're far from our best selves in these moments. We probably are far more impulsive, edgy, aggressive, easily annoyed and set off.

That's stress and anxiety in action.

You get the idea?

Now imagine that dynamic is your constant state. Imagine it being day after day. You'd probably turn into someone you're not super crazy about or proud of. Make sense?

So, now take these dogs we've been talking about. Imagine them - coming with whatever baggage they already have, and then imagine them being in a perpetual state of arousal. Mix the pre-existing issues along with that arousal, and you've got the magic recipe for major trouble.

But what if you could teach these dogs to mentally and physically slow down, relax, and sit tight? If you could teach these overwhelmed guys to just chill, you'd see massive changes. As the arousal fades, you would start to find your dog sharing very different behavior.

Often, just slowing these dogs down, and teaching them to self-regulate, creates almost unrecognizable dogs. The crazy behavior that was so impossible to deal with, has miraculously disappeared. The chronic barking, the obsessive licking, the crazed reactivity, the edgy, dangerous stuff is massively different.

How can just teaching calm create these kinds of profound changes? Simple. Once that aroused state is replaced with calm, your dog is able to access stress and anxiety-free thoughts and actions. A brain that isn't on fire is a brain that makes totally different decisions.

Just like you once the traffic clears, you hit that appointment, and make your way home and relax. How different are you now, now that all that stress and anxiety is off your plate?

My guess would be considerable. And it's the same for your dog.

*To cultivate these calm states, we recommend the structured walk and heel, thresholds exercises at the crate and door, and lots of duration place and down.

STRUCTURE
IN YOUR ABSENCE

Half the battle of training and fixing problem issues is simply preventing the bad habits you're trying to fix from getting practiced.

This can be a challenge. (!)

Dogs left to their own devices will inevitably get into trouble. Barking at windows or gates or doors, freaking out at the mailman or other delivery folks, chasing squirrels, fence fighting, or just staying amped up for hours is going to undo much, if not all, of your hard training work.

That's why we're such big proponents of crates. Crates ensure your dog's mental state is the same as when you left. All the hard work and progress is still there. Safe and sound.

And as the wise Laura Morgan once said, "Crates are structure in your absence." 🐾

slow is **HARD**, fast is EASY

Wanna challenge your dog? Wanna work the brain? Wanna help reduce arousal and over-excitement? Wanna teach your dog to have multiple gears...instead of just one...crazy fast?

If you've got one of those adrenaline junkies who just wants to do everything at light speed (and whose behavior suffers for it), this adjustment can make a huge difference. Start focusing on slowing your dog down.

Instead of zippy recalls, have your dog slowly follow you at a snail's pace.

Instead of speed walks or jogs, walk slooooooow, and challenge your dog to heel right next to you at that pace.

Instead of using a release word (break, free, okay) that's loaded with go-go juice (for thresholds, play, leaving crate, releasing to food), use a new word and condition your dog to a new association.

Instead of allowing constant following, pacing, walking, or running in the house or yard, teach your dog duration "place" command.

Look for moments where your dog tunes out conscious thought and tunes in the crazy, and go after those moments. Look for creative ways to slow them down. You'll see a better state of mind, not just a slower dog.

> You don't need to be perfect to be a great owner and help your dog. If you can hit 80% good stuff, with 20% less-than-perfect stuff, you'll be fine. **Mistakes are gonna happen.** Don't beat yourself up and don't lose hope. Even as professionals we make mistakes every day, but we just move on, and so do the dogs. Do your very best, and let the rest go.
>
> **You'll both be happier and better for it.**

Mirroring is a concept where we teach the dog that good behavior creates comfortable and fun interactions, and negative behavior creates uncomfortable and not fun interactions.

When dogs show up here in a bratty, pushy, disrespectful, or aggressive state, we bring all our resources to bear. Of course we utilize tools, rules, and structure, but one of our secret weapons is using social pressure and contrasts.

What's that look like?

Nasty behavior gets the cold shoulder, zero affection, and air of aloof dislike. (Of course we don't actually dislike the dogs, but that attitude has value of leverage.)

As long as the dog "nasties" continue, so do the nasties from us. But as soon as the dog gives us a change or a break in attitude, we instantly mirror that new positive demeanor. We want to show the dog clear and dramatic contrasts. It's a bit of "see what nice gets," versus "see what nasty gets."

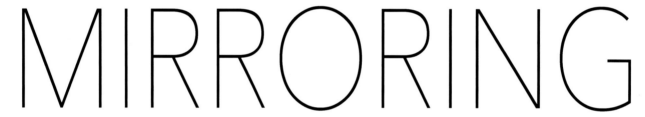

Once dogs become softer and sweeter in attitude, so do we, but not a minute sooner.

Think of it as being both good cop and bad cop all rolled into one. The idea behind good cop/bad cop is to show clear contrasts and options. "We can do this the easy way, or we can do this the hard way" type of stuff.

The social pressure is a motivator. It's another tool to move dogs forward.

A typical mistake I see SO many owners make, along with rescue folks, foster folks, and even other trainers, is to share soft, sweet, affectionate interactions with pushy, bratty, demanding, disrespectful, and even aggressive dogs. Sharing the soft, rewarding, permissive stuff, before the polite, respectful stuff is in place.

That's bad news. And dangerous news.

This is the perfect way to train dogs that these unhealthy behaviors are accepted and desired by you. It leaves dangerous, overly-aroused behaviors unchecked, even

encouraged. And on top of all that great stuff, it also it teaches the dog that you are a soft presence and one that need not be respected or listened to. You basically present yourself as a doormat. And we all know what doormats are for. :)

Giving your soft stuff before getting the dog's soft stuff is an easy mistake to make, and one that can have disastrous, dangerous, or simply counter-productive outcomes.

Instead, learn to mirror the dog's behavior. Give them strong, clear contrasts through what you share. Make sure their good stuff is the price of admission to yours. Become a magnet—an emotional and physiological presence that draws your dog in the direction you want them to go.

But make 'em earn it! :)

stepping UP

Remember guys, dog training, like parenting, isn't supposed to always be a blast.

There's some folks out there trying to make you believe it's always sunshine and rainbows. Everything should always be fun, and dogs should always be smiling. But sometimes the very best, most healthy, positive growth… for dogs and kids…comes not from the fun, joy, and exuberance of all being well.

Often the very best stuff comes from sharing the hard stuff.

The not fun stuff.

The heavy stuff.

The rules stuff.

The accountability stuff.

The unpopular stuff.

You know, the stuff that makes you a great owner or parent.

watch your DOG

There's only one of you who knows what works and what doesn't…

Your dog.

Prong collar too soft or too firm? He'll tell you. E-collar levels too low or too high? He'll tell you. Praise and affection helping or hindering? He'll tell you. Food hyping him up or helping motivate him? He'll tell you. Tone of voice and body language too firm or too passive? He'll tell you.

Don't get hung up on what you think should or shouldn't work, just watch your dog. He knows, and he'll tell you every time.

THE MAGIC OF DURATION WORK

So what's all the fuss about "duration work"? What's the value in having a dog just sit there...for like a long time? How is this going to help my poorly behaved, crazy dog?

Good question. And I've got some good answers for you. :)

Here's the scoop: Dogs get themselves locked in cycles of hyper awareness, hyper reactivity, mental high alert, and edginess. Imagine the overworked Wall Street guy, constantly on edge, anxious, stressed, and overwhelmed. Yep, that's your dog. Or at least most of your dogs.

These dogs spend the majority of their days just like the Wall Street dude. Stressed, edgy, and overwhelmed. Except they're not working on the next trade or watching the numbers. No, your dog is worried about the mailman, the guests coming in the door, why you're walking into the next room, why you're walking out to get the mail. They're worried about the dog next door that's barking at the fence. They're pissed off at the snotty rottie that parades past the large window that faces the front yard. The squirrel that keeps taunting them from the tree. They're concerned about door knocks, noises in the back yard, noises in the front yard...

Get the picture?

We think our dogs are just being dogs. Just hanging out, taking in the world, and reacting accordingly—even normally. What we don't get is that our dogs are spending their days with overloaded minds and overloaded nervous systems.

This creates the edgy, barky, frantic, nervous, growly, overreacting, constantly in motion, freaking out dogs that so many owners struggle with.

These are the dogs making all kinds of poor choices...every day.

And these choices are the results of this daily loading and overwhelm.

So this is where duration work comes in to save the day...and the dog. (And you.) By teaching our dogs the "place" command, or "down-stay," and then slowly working to proof and get your dog into a bomb-proof space with this—meaning he or she can hold the command for as long as needed, regardless of what's going on around them—we can massively help their stress and overwhelm.

And subsequently, their poor behavior.

Think of it as canine meditation. The concept of human meditation is basically the same. Be still, be quiet, watch thoughts and impulses float across your consciousness...and simply let them roll by. Over time, we learn to reprogram our minds and nervous systems to be less reactive and easily triggered. We become more comfortable, less stressed, and better able to successfully navigate our busy worlds.

Sounds good right?

Duration work basically does the same for our dogs. And while we can't control their thoughts, we can control their bodies and their reactions to their environment. Thereby, affecting the mind and body, and ultimately their behavior, in an incredibly positive fashion.

We can help condition them to see and hear all the elements of their world going on around them, and learn to just passively watch or listen. No need to freak out and explode. Slowly, with practice, the triggers of your dog's world lose more and more of their intensity. Eventually, your dog becomes a meditation master. Able to allow all the crazy of the world to simply roll by, without spiking their adrenaline, causing a meltdown, shooting them out of a cannon, and most importantly, helping them to just relax and enjoy the world.

Oh, and to behave as well. :)

As stress levels and anxiety recede, and as your dog develops a new mental and physical default, you'll find that many, if not most of the previous issues you were constantly battling have simply faded away.

The barking dog next door? No biggie. The knock on the door? Yeah, who cares. Guests arriving? Easy breezy. The kid on the skateboard riding by the window? Yeah, so? The frantic, edgy, stressed out dude you used to know has been replaced by an easy, calm, chilled out and comfy dog. A dog with the mental skills to navigate his world and make awesome choices about it.

So that's why all the fuss about duration work.

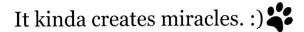

It kinda creates miracles. :)

the MISSING LINK in training

When dogs go home from our board and train program, we always give owners strict guidelines for the next 30-90 days, depending on the severity of the case. Those 30-90 days are absolutely critical.

They either make or break the work and the new beginning you and your dog are embarking on.

This is where so many training programs fall short. Why do they fall apart, even after good training? Because the trainer has been living with the dog in a very specific way. This way of living together has created the foundation for a healthy, respectful relationship. And this relationship is exactly what empowers or disempowers all the training.

The trainer turns over a well-trained dog. A dog that knows the commands, the rules, the expectations, the consequences, and the dynamic of the relationship...with that trainer. Unfortunately, that well-trained dog still has all of their old perceptions, associations, and feelings about its owner.

This is the relationship dynamic. And this relationship dynamic—the way the dog feels about you—will always trump standard obedience work alone. Why? Because the feeling the dog has about the owner will often overpower and override commands and tools. Disrespect is a powerful thing.

Of course, obedience commands that are asked for and enforced will go a long way towards changing and affecting your relationship. Your dog will see and hear you ask things of them, and if consequences are shared for non-compliance, they will learn you mean business. And that will create a healthy, valuable impact.

But there are other aspects of your time spent together with your dog, beyond the obedience work, that if leveraged, along with everything else, will give you a much greater chance of success. And if ignored, will likely mean trouble.

So in order to fix this essential piece of the training puzzle, we've developed some highly effective protocols. Ways of living with your dog that go beyond simple obedience that work to overhaul your relationship. These are the ways we've lived with your dog to create the results we've obtained.

Ready for the puzzle piece?

Restrictions.

Restrictions are likely a big part of what your trainer used to help create a positive, healthy, respectful relationship. Smart trainers restrict and control movement, affection, food, and even play. They control what the dog experiences and make it clear that permission for all these valued things comes directly from them.

These restrictions create a framework for respect and healthy perceptions. Perceptions that go far beyond just obedience work. They're part of the bigger picture of creating a healthy relationship.

Why are these restrictions so important? Because a dog who is allowed to roam freely feels very different than a dog whose freedom comes from their owner. A dog who receives tons of unearned affection feels very different than a dog who has to earn it through awesome behavior. A dog who has access to food at any time feels different than a dog whose food comes when their owner shares it with them. And a dog who plays whenever it wants to feels very different than a dog who is given permission about when it is and isn't play time.

All these are incredibly important conversations, especially in the beginning when owners are trying to create new feelings and associations. Do we have to live with our dogs like this forever? Probably not. That's largely determined by your dog and you. And as always, the more convincingly you kick butt, in general, the more latitude you typically get. But until you have amazing stuff coming from your dog, consistently and for a long time, I wouldn't even think about removing these.

But I would think of them, in the long term, as something flexible, depending on how things develop. A means to an end. Something you get to adjust as a reward, for you and your dog, for good work done.

Here's a list for the TGD reboot program. Hopefully, the specifics help you guys put all the pieces together:

- Dog sleeps in crate.
- Dog is in crate whenever you're gone, or he/she is unsupervised.
- Dog is only out of the crate when working, training, walking, or pottying.
- Withhold all affection. (For now!)
- Treat the dog in an aloof, distant fashion.
- Don't play or horse around with your dog.
- Practice tons of duration "place" or "down" work (your dog can be in one spot for several hours).
- Use obedience commands (recall, sit, down, heel, crate, thresholds, etc.) to ask things of your dog that reinforce a leadership-based relationship.
- Don't just do what's easy. Challenge your dog to do what's difficult—whether that's "placing" somewhere challenging or recalling past scary or enticing things.
- Always be working on duration, distance, and distraction to proof and grow your training.
- No free feeding. Your dog eats when it's feeding time, and the bowl is removed 5 minutes later—even if the dog doesn't eat or finish.
- The walk is highly structured. No marking, sniffing, wandering, or pulling. Your dog walks in "heel" 90% of the time and is allowed to potty/sniff 10% of the time, and only on your release.
- All negative behavior (barking, whining, growling, jumping, breaking command) is corrected firmly.

These are the restrictions and actions we've used to get over a thousand dogs into a great space. They'll work for you too.

Remember, relationship - the way your dog feels about you - takes time to overhaul. Old memories and feelings don't just up and disappear. They and you need time and every advantage you can utilize for success. Leverage all these recommendations and you should see some amazing changes.

While our clients love it, we catch a fair amount of friction from others for our lack of consistent use of food in our training program.

Many feel there's nothing in it for the dog, and that it creates less enthusiastic, less "happy" dogs. And I get it. Using food will typically create a more "happy" appearance. But that appearance—the overly attentive, juiced up, "what's next," on-edge dog—isn't the kind of dog we like to send home.

While it looks great in videos, in my opinion, it's not always the best thing for dogs and their owners. Let me explain:

WHEN WE USE **FOOD** AND WHY

So many dogs struggle with arousal, excitement, or impulse control issues, and bringing food into the mix can increase these issues. And many dogs struggle with attitude issues, and paying for (rather than requiring) compliance can have adverse effects here as well.

Those dogs who struggle with arousal, excitement, or impulse control issues can be turned into edgy, overly-attentive, hyped-up machines who become more problematic with food in play. And those with attitude issues who feel the world is theirs, who love to push boundaries, and have little respect for people, will often feel more entitled (and less "required"). So for us, in these situations, using food would be counterproductive.

So we forgo it.

The situations in which we do use food would be for those dogs that are slow movers (dogs that aren't excited about working, who are mopey, etc), dogs who are highly human-aggressive (with which we need to leverage food and resources to create a bridge to seeing us in a new fashion), and dogs who are super shut down (super fearful dogs who will benefit from feeling excited or happy about training, life, and us).

For these guys, we see using food as a definite benefit, and so we use it and then fade it out.

Our goal here at TGD is to send home dogs who are their very best versions of themselves. We want to send home relaxed, calm, easy-going dogs. Dogs who are respectful, safe, polite, reliable, and happy - in the best sense of the word. We train dogs to live the way we live with our own dogs here.

I personally don't want my dogs constantly waiting on the next payday, watching my every move to see if it's command time or food time, or shaking me down for some action. I just want them to hang out and relax. So that's what we shoot for with our client dogs.

There's nothing wrong using food to train dogs. It can be a game changer and life saver. But I've also seen plenty of dogs where using food made them worse, not better.

My recommendation would be to use food in a simple fashion: **when it helps.**

When it helps a dog to make better choices. When it helps to make a dog feel better and perform better. When it helps a dog to transform. But leave it out when it makes it harder for the dog. When it fogs the mind with arousal. When it makes relaxing difficult. When it makes a dog edgy and fixated. 🐾

P.S. Just to clarify, this is our philosophy, our belief about what we want to see in our dogs that we train. If you use food with your dogs—whether you're an owner or trainer—and you or your clients dig the results, then that's awesome! Keep on doing your thing. I just want to clarify our take on using food, and what's behind our thought process.

INTRODUCING NEW DOGS TO THE PACK

What's the best way to introduce a new dog to my dog or dogs?

This is one of the questions we get most often. Introducing dogs and helping them to peacefully co-exist can be a major challenge. With so many nuances in play, and so many opportunities to make mistakes, it's an easy one to struggle with.

Whether you're adopting a new dog for yourself, doing foster work, or just having a friend or family member's dog over, there are some solid ways to go about this, and there are some ways that are perfect setups for disaster.

Here's a list of what we've found to work best, and what to watch out for. Be aware that these are macro, all-encompassing principles, not a step-by-step introduction process.

- Create an atmosphere of rules, structure, and leadership. This atmosphere will pull the best out of dogs and discourage their less-best. Meaning, if you actually share rules, structure, and lead with believability, dogs will make their best choices. This is where all the good stuff or bad stuff starts. We all know when a leader is present, and we behave accordingly. If you understand this concept, you're way ahead of the game...and have a much better chance of success.

- Don't create excitement. Understand that excitement—play, affection, high-pitched, excited talk—is often the gateway to elevated states in dogs. These elevated states are almost always present when dogs get into trouble. When working on introducing dogs, remember that calm and cool are always your best friends.

- Don't create competition. Dogs are super happy to fight over resources. Food, toys, chews, affection, furniture, and proximity to you (being on or near you) are the most common triggers, but there can be far more.

- Don't be in a rush. The biggest cause of dog fights and scuffles are from owners moving too fast. Time is often your biggest aid. Just allowing the novelty of newness to wear off can make things so much easier. Be aware that novelty creates excitement, concern, stress, anxiety. So move slow.

- Make sure your own dog or dogs are well-behaved. If you're starting with a mess you've got an awfully good chance of having a bigger mess when you bring another dog into the mix. If your dogs are frantic, pushy, demanding, bullying, possessive, and out of their trees, the chance of having problems are extremely high. Make sure your dogs are polite, chilled out, listening to you, and as calm as can be initially.

- Make sure the newcomer is well-behaved. If you bring a frantic, pushy, demanding, bullying, possessive, out-of-its-tree dog into your home or yard you've got a very high probability of your dogs disagreeing with the new dog. Fights or scuffles are almost guaranteed.

- Don't introduce them. Yep, you heard me. The best way for dogs to feel comfortable and develop positive feelings towards each other is to simply exist around each other. Think of existence as a low-stress introduction, and think of actually meeting and interacting as a high-stress introduction.

The longer you allow them to just exist around each other, the better your chances of a "no big deal" actual meeting. The more they see each other without interacting, the less they care about each other. (How? Place command, walking together, or in crates around each other.)

- Be aware and honest with yourself if you have a resource guarder, scrapper, ultra-dog-insecure, or bully in your crew. This has to be dealt with or managed heavily to avoid fallout. Don't live in denial or make excuses. If you do, you'll find that the dogs will reveal the truth pretty quickly. Be honest and address it, or suffer the consequences.

- Use crates whenever leaving dogs unattended. Do not leave dogs alone together who are new to each other...even for brief moments. Even if they've been angels in your presence. In your absence many things (door bells, delivery people, a squirrel or cat in the yard, objects or spaces in the house) can trigger competition or over-arousal...and fights.

- Don't feed dogs close together. Never feed new dogs out of the crate near each other. This is an easy one to understand (it's dog fight central). Also, don't feed in crates near each other without something separating and obscuring the view of each other. Even in crates, and even from across the room, a dog could feel threatened or competitive when eating. Once out, that tension could create a fight...or a slow-building grudge.

- Address crappy behavior immediately and firmly...from any party. Whether it's your dog or the newcomer, if someone is being a brat or demanding, or a bully, or just posturing, tense, or stink-eyeing, address it straight away! Don't let the dogs feel they have to handle it. It's your job to keep the peace and set the tone. Do it, or the dogs will.

- Don't just toss dogs together and cross your fingers that it'll all be cool. Often it won't. This is the "Hail Mary," lazy, uninformed move, and should be avoided at all costs.

- Learn to trust your gut. This means, don't just look at the surface with the dogs. How does it feel? Is there tension? Are there nuances of crappiness? Or are things feeling relaxed and comfortable? Without a professional guiding you, you'll have to become the person to judge this. You're able to feel these nuances in people. That means you can develop the same ability with dogs...if you really work at it.

- Hire a professional to help guide you. Be sure he or she is actually familiar with this kind of work. Ask them what their approach would be. If it goes against the principles listed here, I'd look elsewhere.

While all this might sound like overkill, I assure you, after seeing hundreds of fighting dogs come through TGD, this is the stuff—done, or not done—that typically creates the problems. Also understand that starting off right is about 4 bazillion times easier than trying to fix relationships that have gone south. Understand that grudges aren't just for humans. Dogs build and act out on grudges, just like we do. Once built, they're extremely hard to dismantle. You're much better off taking the slow, overly-cautious, "overkill" approach and never needing to see a behavior mod specialist, than you are rushing things.

Be aware, any time you bring dogs together who are unfamiliar with each other, you run the risk of trouble. This is serious stuff and demands a serious approach.

RECIPROCAL PLAY

What's cool and what's not?

Is my dog okay?

Is the other dog okay?

Are they fighting or playing?

When do you stop it and when do you allow it?

When it comes to dogs playing it can be hard to discern what's okay and what's not—what's healthy and what's harmful.

We use a term called "Reciprocal Play" to help owners understand what we generally look for. What is it? Basically, the concept is to look at both dogs and see if things are balanced. Are they going back and forth? Is one chasing the other and tackling, pawing, mouthing...and then is this reversing? Is the chaser the chasee?

What we're really looking to prevent is a one-sided interaction. We don't want one dog chasing, pawing, tackling, mouthing...bullying...while the other dog is overwhelmed, freaked out, and wanting to escape. This is how fights and reactive, nervous dogs are created. We're looking for both dogs to be enjoying the interaction.

And just to be clear, this can look and sound pretty rough, depending on the dogs. So don't let sound and appearance determine your reaction alone. Also, some dogs enjoy being chased more than chasing, and some enjoy being roughed up more than doing the roughing.

Evaluating play is a nuanced thing for sure. Different dogs will bring out different play and behavior in your dog.

The best way to determine if things are cool is to watch the big picture, not just one intense moment, and look to see if both dogs are enjoying and coming back for more. 🐾

THE ESCALATION SEQUENCE

Depending on your dog, it can take a few seconds or a blink of an eye. What is it? It's the mental and physiological sequence that your dog goes through when something valuable occurs.

And just to clarify, valuable doesn't mean good, just important.

It could be something scary (someone skateboarding towards you, a dog on-leash barking, a trash truck, a stranger, etc.), it could be something exciting (a squirrel darting out, a knock on the front door, the jingle of the leash, etc.), or it could be something that creates conflict (guarding a toy, food, space, or person, etc.).

Regardless of where it comes from emotionally, there's a sequence. Awareness of the trigger (what's that?), evaluation of the trigger (should I do something?), and reaction to the trigger (kaboom!).

Your dog's specific personality (easy-going or pushy), drives (prey, toy, food, attention), strengths (confidence and resiliency), weaknesses (fearfulness and insecurity), along with the proximity and intensity of the trigger, will determine how fast this sequence goes and how long you have to react to it.

Think about this sequence on a scale of one to ten. The only time you have to actually block, stop, or correct a reaction is typically between 1-3, maybe 4, if you're lucky. Once you get to the 5's and beyond, it's almost always too late, and at this point trying to address the moment usually just makes it worse.

Regardless of the dog, this sequence usually flies by, and most owners struggle with being waaaaay behind their dog's response, or sequence.

The trick is being aware of the sequence, being aware of the triggers, being aware of your specific dog, and getting ahead of the reaction. You've got a teeny moment in time to correct and have an impact. After that, it's too late.

Get ahead of the sequence, and you'll be set to actually teach your dog to make a better choice. Get behind the sequence and you'll have to wait until next time. 🐾

LIVING TRAINING

You don't do training, you live training.

Training isn't a task or a regimen or set of commands, it's a lifestyle. Training is a way of living and being with our dogs. It's a 24/7 thing.

When we get out of the mode of "training time" and get into the mode of "training life", we catch all the moments. We provide the consistency and continuous presence needed for our dogs to thrive.

HOW DO YOU GET A **BETTER DOG?**

Answer: the same way you get a better body, better relationships, better finances, better career, and a better attitude and outlook on life. You work on it daily.

Yep, that's it.

Okay, let's break it down just a little more. All of these pursuits, which include your dog, are improved by steady, disciplined, informed action. If you take steady, disciplined, informed action daily, you will get results. Period.

There's no mystery, no elusive secret.

Making progress, moving forward, and transforming any aspect of your life isn't really complicated. It's actually pretty straightforward. But what IS hard is the consistency. The sticking with it. The effort, day in and day out. The doing, even when you want to be doing something else.

This focus on consistent daily work and small, incremental progress is the only form of magic involved. And isn't it good news that there's no magic at play? That's it's all controllable?

It's up to each of us to decide how badly we want (and how hard we're willing to work for) whatever it is we desire from this life. The sky is pretty much the limit.

If you want that beautiful body, you can have it. If you want a fulfilling career, you can have it. If you want an amazing relationship, you can have it. If you want to be financially rocking, you can have it. If you want a great attitude, you can have it. And if you want a great dog, you can have that too.

No magic, no mysteries.

Just focus, priorities, sacrifice, desire, and hard freaking daily work.

DOG TRAINING
1 0 1

I know this might sound overly simplistic, but it's often super helpful to take complex concepts and find ways to turn them on their heads to make them as simple and accessible as possible.

Whatever the training, whatever the issue is, whatever the behavior you're working on, this is the formula: if it's pulling on the leash, make pulling uncomfortable and not pulling comfortable. If it's jumping on people, make jumping uncomfortable and not jumping comfortable. If it's recall, make not recalling uncomfortable and recalling comfortable.

How you go about doing both of these depends on the tools and methods you subscribe to, but at the end of the day, this is all the complex, fancy training stuff distilled down to its most basic, tangible, and effective principles. 🐾

TRY IT!!

We just had a shadow student here for 5 days of intensive training with the TGD team and me.

We handled a bunch of dogs, all at different points of development in training (from totally green to beginning E-collar), and all with different attitudes, issues, and challenges.

The thing I found us sharing with the shadow student more than anything else was the constant need for creativity. Not that she wasn't creative (she was) but even with a creative mind it's still easy to get locked into protocols, blueprints, and methodology.

Here at TGD we have a definite training blueprint we use as guideline with all dogs that come through here. We typically start all dogs a certain way, move through certain phases of training in a certain fashion, and so on. But we're also super open-minded to shaking things up. Perhaps the most important part of being a great trainer is being open, creative, and solution-focused. The ability to deviate, to experiment, to totally jettison a usually successful technique or approach in favor of something better, for the specific dog in front of you.

As we were working with all the dogs, and if she got stuck on some behavior or exercise, I'd say, "try____." If we were on pressure with E-collar and the dog was struggling to down with low pressure, I might suggest a quick tap instead of holding continuous. Or a slightly higher level, or a slightly lower level, or changing her body position, or…

So often the answer was off the beaten path. So often what worked was NOT what we typically recommend or teach. Sometimes it was the exact opposite. It was great for the shadow student to see how often the answer was something not in the standard playbook of typical steps or typical answers.

This is what makes dog training so fun and so challenging. And it's a great reminder for all you trainers and owners out there. Even if you've seen a great step-by-step example or the perfect blueprint to getting a dog trained for whatever (even if you're following our DVDs!!), remember; stay super open-minded, be willing to switch it up and if something's not working, try something else. Get creative. Break some rules.

The cool thing is, if it doesn't work, you can always try something else. Explore a little. You're not going to destroy your dog or his or her training with a little experimentation, or even a mistake.

But if you stay super rigid and refuse to deviate from a blueprint or protocol, you and your dog could remain stuck and struggling. 🐾

OWN IT!!

The dog-owning and dog-training world is, unfortunately, chock full of generously judgmental folks.

People who will happily (and without invitation) share their opinions and judgments in regards to your dog, your training, and of course the tools you choose to use.

I've met so many owners and trainers who have been shamed, blamed, belittled, chastised, yelled at, and even threatened for their training approach with their dogs.

We're talking about smart, nice, conscientious owners and trainers getting some incredibly nasty stuff from those who don't approve. Critics who have taken it upon themselves to determine what everyone else should (or shouldn't) be doing.

And of course at the top of the list of tools that are the most vilified and nasty are the prong and E-collar.

These tools are framed as being only capable of abuse. Tools that are used by cruel, lazy people. People looking for shortcuts. People who don't care about their dogs. People who are happy to blast or yank their dogs into good behavior.

But the funny thing is, I've seen the exact opposite. I haven't seen the abuse, the carelessness, the casualness, the callousness. Instead, I've seen owners far more cautious and careful with the E-collar. I've seen owners constantly needing coaching to dial up, not down. I've seen owners apprehensive to give their dogs a firm pop on the prong collar, needing us to remind them it isn't going to harm their dog.

So how come these tools of abuse aren't being used to torture and ruin dogs?

Why? Because most owners are really great people. They're caring, kind people who only want the best for their dogs. They're great people looking for answers and help. People looking for tools that will help them keep their dogs in their home, keep their dogs safe, and allow them to include their dog in their lives in a much greater fashion.

But that's not what certain groups of people want you to believe. They want to convince you that only nasty, lazy, cruel folks would use these tools. That's the agenda. That's the message.

If you're one of these committed, hard-working, caring owners who are working your rears off to have the best dog you can, to have the most freedom and fun you can...I highly suggest you own your tools and approach, without apology. Ignore the shame and blame game, ignore the haters and uninformed. Let the nastiness and ignorance fall on deaf ears. Don't you dare let these people bully you into feeling bad about how you train your dogs and what tools you use. Do your research, learn the skills, make your decisions based on proof and results, and then...own it!!

is your dog TOO SMART for training?

Relationships are real things.

You and your dog have one.

It might be healthy, balanced, and awesome, or it might be toxic, disrespectful, and disheartening. Or maybe it's somewhere in between. Whatever it is, it's been built by your interactions. What you've allowed. What you haven't allowed. What you've asked for. What you've reinforced. Who you've been and how you've behaved.

Everything you've done has been information your dog has used to determine your relationship. All this information has told your dog who you are and what role you wish to play in his life. It's also informed him about the rules of life. What is and isn't okay, what is and isn't expected. It's created the framework your dog makes all his decisions from.

While trainers can teach your dog commands, manners, and what is and isn't acceptable behavior, your dog is simply too smart and too emotionally evolved to take that information as universal. Just like you know who means business and who doesn't in your own life, so does your dog. Eventually, if you don't keep up the work, if you start to slack, your dog will see the cracks. He'll realize there's two sets of rules: the ones you enforce, and the ones you don't. And he'll choose the latter. Not because he's a bad dog, but because he's opportunistic ... just like you and me.

Like us, when authority and rules are foggy and not consistently enforced, we tend to take advantage of them. Whether we like to admit it or not, it's always consequences–or the possibility of them–that tends to keep us on our best behavior. The more predictable and dependable, the better our behavior tends to be. And of course, the less predictable and dependable, the worse our behavior tends to be.

Our dogs are reading us. All the time. What are we enforcing, what are we allowing? They're taking this information and deciding what needs to be adhered to and what doesn't, who needs to be listened to and who doesn't. If you ask for less than what the trainer asked, you'll get less. If you ask the same, you'll get the same. It's in these moments that you create your relationship dynamics.

And while us trainers can build the foundation for new, more healthy patterns and choices to stand on, it's only you–the person your dog lives with, the person who enforces the rules, structure, and expectations daily–that can make these changes permanent.

We can only give you the tools to start you on the path; we can't build the relationship. That part, the hard part, is up to you. Your dog is too smart to have it any other way.

Lots of folks ask about confidence-building exercises for shy or fearful dogs. This can be a challenging endeavor.

So much of it depends on the dog herself. How genetically sound is she? How much early exposure did she get or not get?

All dogs can improve, but we might bump into some serious limitations.

That said, there are lots of theories and approaches out there. Some subscribe to having the dog do challenging agility work. Some look for fear-inducing situations and work to slowly get the dog to overcome their concerns. Most do some form of obedience commands in conjunction with the above.

Here at TGD, our basic concept is to get the dog to listen to the training, rather than to their fear, concerns, worries. I know that sounds simple, but when done in a very specific fashion, it creates amazing results.

A big part of the magic of this approach is our choice of tools: using an E-collar to teach, proof, and work dogs through trouble spots.

Why E-collar, especially with nervous, insecure, fearful dogs? Because it is, without question, the most amazing tool for these guys.

Here's why: with other tools, the dog feels they're being forced to do the activity. This just creates more stress, more resistance, and more fear. With the E-collar, when done correctly, the dog feels they're doing the work. They feel they're recalling towards the scary person that, a few minutes ago, they wanted to run from. Are you actually compelling them to recall? Yep. But in the dog's mind, the perception is different.

Same goes for other commands. Eventually, there's no leash or long line attached. The dog sits, downs, recalls, heels, etc., all on its own. The E-collar is there to help if the dog gets confused or overwhelmed, but once again the dog feels that she's the one finding the courage to complete the exercise. (Many folks will want to argue with this approach, asserting that the dog is performing out of fear, but we have so many videos showing otherwise, that the argument is moot.)

Some will ask, if the goal is to have the dog "feel" they're doing the work, and humans aren't forcing them to do it, then why not just do food training?

confidence

Good question.

And there's a simple answer. True insecurity, nervousness, and fear are such powerful emotional states that food has no value. You can wave a steak in front of a freaked out dog, and she won't want anything to do with it. So then what?

So for us, the answer to building confidence is just our usual program. A program built on listening to the training and listening to the human. Performing commands (eventually) without a leash, and plenty of options to do otherwise. And having commands being performed and proofed through ever-challenging levels of distraction and triggers.

Building towards non-negotiable commands, solid leadership, and using tools that make the dog feel empowered and confident is how we do our thing with these challenging dogs.

SLEUTHING

You can't get caught up in assessing a dog with just the current moment.

So many owners and trainers tend to make determinations on a dog's intent, ability, and actions based solely on what's occurring in the moment in front of them. What the dog is offering here and now. But that's just a snapshot in time, and it can be super misleading.

To be truly effective with dogs you gotta go deeper. You gotta become an emotional, behavioral, and attitude sleuth.

This means you take into account ALL the preceding behavior, ALL the past moments, and use ALL the information to help you determine what exactly is cooking.

Have you seen pushy, snotty, tense, guarding, or disrespectful behavior prior? If you have, that doesn't live in a vacuum. It's part of the dog, and it's part of the dog's emotional, behavioral, attitude, repertoire.

The wise trainer or owner sees it all and factors it all in. They know to look for the big picture, not just the current one. They use that info to make wiser, deeper, far more informed choices. Choices that tend to take into account the entire dog.

Of course, this doesn't mean that once a dog does something that they're always that dog. Specific factors and triggers in that moment could bring things to the fore, things that aren't necessarily permanent red flags. But, they should always be in the back of your mind as possibilities...and information you use to get to the bottom of things.

Dogs are both clever creatures and open books. They will inadvertently tip their hands in a moment—if you're looking—and then conceal that behavior or choice in another. Crafty...and obvious!

What might this look like? A dog comes in that I've seen video of with him bullying his owner. Later, I see him try to blow out of the crate or through a threshold or jump on me in a very specific way, with a very specific flavor. (Bully and bratty flavor!) Then, when I'm working with the dog on recall or place, I keep seeing the dog blow it. He keeps messing up some very simple training steps.

Do we have a learning issue or do we have an attitude issue?

Factoring in all the previous info—and being acutely tuned-in to the "feel" of the choices and actions taken—will help you make an informed decision.

But if you just look at the moment in front of you, you could be easily bamboozled.

Confusion or choice? That's an important question you should always be asking yourself, and info you should be looking for.

If you really focus on becoming sensitive to body language, eye contact (or lack of), the "feel" of the dog, and whether the dog has a clear head or lives in a state of overwhelm, AND if you pair all of that info with all the previous behavior shared, you should be able to get a pretty accurate picture of the dog.

And what will best serve him.

More reps or more accountability? Backing off a bit or adding more pressure?

Dogs, like us, have attitudes, desires, and agendas. And like us, if you watch them long enough, you'll start to see the truth. The cracks will start to show. And that deeper, more nuanced and sleuthy approach to reading and problem solving will help you make the very best decisions based on the entire dog, not just the moment.

putting out the fire

Lots of talk about the fallout from correcting dogs around things they're excited, worried, or fearful of.

The messages are built around the idea that you will create a negative association by correcting around one of these triggers.

The real bummer is that these messages are so ubiquitous that many owners have bought into them.

So they're afraid to correct their dogs. Instead, they work to counter-condition and create "positive" associations through food and other rewards.

What they're missing, and not being told, is that the negative association is already in play. That's why your dog is reacting! If there was no negative association, you wouldn't be seeing any of the issues.

The other part they're missing, and not being told, is that you can't create a positive association while the dog is freaking out over the negative one. First, you've got to stop the negative reaction. Second, you've got to correct and create a calm, more neutral state of mind, THEN you can teach a new way to feel.

You have to block the old to create a gateway for the new.

So the big takeaways:

1) Correcting your dog around triggers won't create negative associations, but it will create the opportunity for new, positive ones. (I've trained too many dogs with reactivity issues, and have yet to see this phenomenon.)

2) Trying to build a house on top of a burning foundation, or trying to teach a tantrumming child to read, or trying to get a freaking-out dog to feel better while it's freaking out...doesn't work.

First stop the issue, knowing you won't make it worse THEN work on creating new feelings.

Once the fire is out, you can build something pretty awesome.

Patience and consistent effort can work **miracles.**

DESMOND

When we got Desmond, we were new dog owners and had no clue what we were in for with regards to training.

We both grew up with Golden Retrievers and thought that we could figure out the German Shepherd breed easily. We had no idea how different the experience would be and how much training was needed to support a shepherd. Due to him getting his first round of shots too early, we were instructed to push back his shot schedule, and keep him inside our house until he was completely up to date. He got plenty of exercise in our yard, and we had lots of people over so he could get socialized the only we way we knew how. The second we got the OK from the vet to take him on walks and bring him out into the open, we realized what a massive mistake this all was, as he was highly aggressive towards dogs on the leash and just overall anxious in the outside world.

He would pull, lunge, bark, growl, snarl, at anything and everything on the walk—cars, motorcycles, people, children, dogs behind fences, dogs on-leash—everything. We had him on a harness and tried distracting him with treats, but, of course, nothing worked. We had these dreams of living our life with our dog, but instead, we couldn't include him in anything. We were devastated.

Over the next year, things got progressively worse. He aggressively growled, barked and nipped at other dogs and our vet. At home, things were no different. When we tried to get Desmond off the bed or inside the house after playing ball he would growl, snarl, bare his teeth, and nip. He had major anxiety when we were gone, and he would chew and bite himself so excessively that he wouldn't sleep. He would pace and whine in the car, and obsessively dig holes in the yard. He aggressively barked at guests coming to our house, and any neighbors or sounds outside. Desperate to change things before they got even worse, we searched and searched for answers, and eventually found The Good Dog. We set up a board and train and finally felt like there was light at the end of the tunnel.

During the board and train, we watched Desmond's transformation on The Good Dog's videos. We couldn't believe that our Desmond was actually walking down 3rd Street Promenade in Santa Monica, with all the people and dogs, not reacting or aggressing. He was listening to commands and he seemed like a happier dog. He was comfortable in his own fur and finding his way. We diligently did our homework, learning the ins and outs of the E-collar, and learning what changes we would need to make in our relationship with Des so that when he came home we could carry on all of the work. We studied the rules and understood that the changes that needed to be made were not just with him, but with us.

The work paid off.

When Desmond came home, he was a new dog. He was still the goofy, fun guy that we fell in love with, but now his anxiety and aggression was non-existent, and he actually listened to us. We could walk him down the street without him reacting and pulling, and we could have people and dogs over for the first time without fear of him nipping or growling. We finally had our lives back and started to enjoy him and his company.

All we wanted to do was have a safe dog that we could live our lives with, but we ended up with so much more. In a reality, we never thought would exist, we are now able to take Desmond on hikes without being terrified of him freaking out when seeing another dog or person. We are able to take Desmond to grab a coffee and brunch, and he sits calmly at our feet, comfortable and relaxed no matter the environment. We are finally living our lives with him, our best dog friend.

We moved to a new house, and Desmond has been so great. Our new neighbors met him about 2 weeks in to us moving and were shocked we had a dog. They said they never hear him during the day when we are gone. He has been a total dream when we go up to Tyler's parents' house, splashing in the water and playing with their dog, but settling down in a place when needed. He runs every morning with me and has now run four dog-friendly 10K races. The Good Dog changed our lives. ## We have never been happier, and Desmond gets better and better every day. He is the best version of himself and makes our family complete.

I know we're always talking about what works best, what tools are best, and what training approach is best, but we haven't talked much about when it's best to stop.

Here's what I mean. When you're teaching your dog a new behavior or working through a problem issue, there always comes a time when you should stop.

The problem is knowing when. It can be easy to see a dog mildly stressed with learning, a bit of confusion, and then throw in the towel. Now that might be the right choice, or it might be that you were climbing the mountain and almost to the top, but then stopped, and will possibly have to start over again at the bottom. (This is especially true for working to extinguish problem behaviors, more so than teaching a new exercise.)

Unfortunately, I can't tell you when the right moment to stop is, or whether continuing might offer the breakthrough you're looking for. All I can do is make some suggestions.

when to STOP

When teaching sit, down, place, recall, heel, etc., it's always preferable to stop on a great moment. But sometimes these moments aren't obvious, or our dogs are struggling, and there's no great moment to be found. When you've got a ton of dog experience, you tend to be able to read when it's worth continuing and when it's time to say whoa. But when you're starting out, or have limited experience, it can be really hard to read.

When you start to see your dog moving backwards in the learning process—making more mistakes than progress—I'd stop. If your dog is looking frantic and wide-eyed, I'd stop. If the tongue is spatulate (wide and hanging dramatically), I'd stop. When you're stressed, frustrated, or annoyed, I'd stop. Look for mental or physical fatigue—from either of you—and look to stop BEFORE that happens.

It's obviously a nuanced and complex situation, but I at least want all of you thinking about stress levels and how too much pressure can inhibit learning rather than enhancing it. Of course, never pushing your dog's comfort zone is also counter-productive.

Finding the balance and being super sensitive AND strong is the magic balance point.

THE ART OF **NOT CARING**
ABOUT DOG TRAINING

There's an interesting thing that great dog trainers do when working with clients that are struggling with their dog.

And what is this "thing"?

They work to get their client to not care about the training. They work to take their client's mind off the dog training. That's right. Instead of getting an owner to focus more intensely on the dog training, they go the other direction. They work hard to get the owner to think about anything else but their dog.

Now, this might sound like it would be counterproductive, but when we hyper-fixate, over-focus, and put too much pressure on ourselves, a whole bunch of stuff transpires.

We get into that over-focused/fixated place; we lose our relaxed body language and become tense. Our breathing changes. We release stress hormones that our dogs smell. We unconsciously apply tension to the leash. Our muscles lose their relaxed elasticity. Our minds become stressed and start to make poorer and poorer choices. We tighten up. We go from natural, unconscious movement to highly conscious movement (which is always bad!!). We start to anticipate issues and telegraph that to our dogs through minute or overt reactions.

By focusing too hard on the training, and all our actions in it, we end up messing the whole thing up. Like anything we try too hard at, we lose our naturalness.

All of these moments start in our minds. They start with our thoughts—our fears, our worries, our anticipating, our focus. And even though we may be doing all the mechanics "right,"—meaning we're correcting when we should correct, using space as a buffer, using enough pressure to be valuable to our dogs, telling ourselves to stay relaxed, and utilizing the tools as instructed—our minds have already betrayed us.

And this mental betrayal can easily override all the good stuff you're actually doing.

That's really the secret: You can't use all the mechanics and be successful without also using the right mindset. One empowers or disempowers the other.

It's all about figuring out how to remove pressure from yourself, rather than add it.

So that's why many great trainers will work hard to get their clients to talk about anything else BUT training. They'll tell them jokes, ask about their work or family. They'll get 'em talking—and more importantly thinking!—about something else. Once the mind lets go of the "battle" at hand, and stops worrying and freaking out, it's free to relax, access its best stuff, and of course, cause your body to respond similarly.

Now, this doesn't mean we just walk out willy-nilly, and not care about the training. It's really a tightrope walk. It's this magic space where you're highly conscious of what your goals are, but you're allowing your mind and body to work in their better, automatic state. The magic space of awareness without mental micro-management and hyper-vigilance. Caring a lot without caring too much. And I call it a magical space because it's just that. But it takes work to find this space.

Even if you're not working with a professional trainer, you could take a friend out on a walk with you to keep you relaxed and not overly dog-focused. You could work on positive self-talk—meaning keeping yourself light and easy. Reminding yourself that it's "just dog training." Remembering to keep things in perspective. Mentally allowing yourself and your dog to be ok to screw up. (Giving yourself and your dog permission to be imperfect can be a huge gift!) You could replay in your mind your favorite comedy movie. Meditate before the walk. Anything that keeps your mind easy and relaxed so it can do its best stuff.

And if you can keep your mind at ease (which will keep your body at ease) while simultaneously doing the mechanics right, you'll likely see a dramatic change in your dog's performance.

Care a lot...
While not caring at all.

That is magic. :)

the checklist

Here's a quick little checklist that we utilize here at TGD. We believe if you adhere to it you can make amazing stuff happen with your own dog!

1) Personal Mindset: We all know that what we carry around and share with the world, impacts those around us. There's no getting by this one. If you're emotionally a mess—if you're needy, dependent, permissive, overly-anxious, constantly stressed, frustrated, or struggle with anger or patience issues,—you're likely going to have a very hard time with your dog. That doesn't mean you have to be perfect. None of us are. We're all a mess from time to time. But if it's a chronic, ongoing dysfunctional or toxic state you're sharing, it's going to affect your dog. Along with that, being in a compromised state will make it exceptionally hard for your dog to listen, respect, and give you his or her best stuff. People in a bad space struggle to have their dogs follow them. You don't have to be perfect, but you do have to be honest...and working on it.

2) The Right Tools: While the tools you use are a personal choice, this is the TGD list, so we'll share what we find to be most helpful and effective. We use E-collar for interior work,

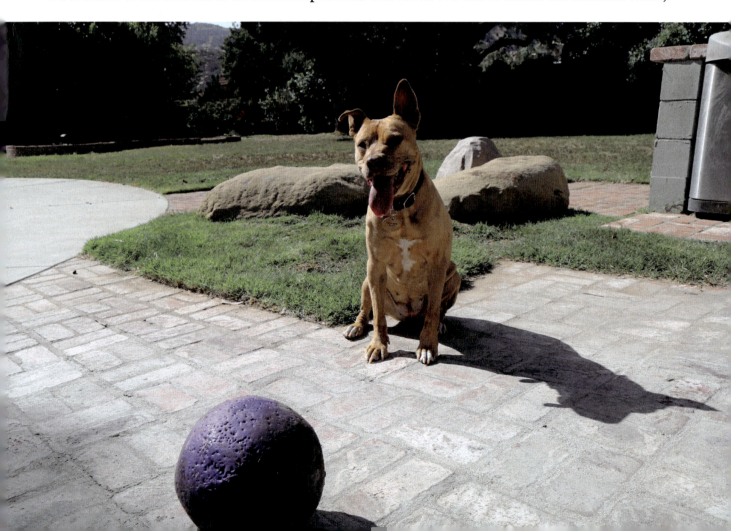

off-leash hikes or excursions, and for walks. Think of the E-collar as an invisible leash, and one that allows you to communicate with your dog up to a mile away. We also use prong collars. We use prongs for teaching basic obedience, as well as for extra safety, control, and direction on walks (along with the E-collar). We also use food and play and affection as part of our training process when appropriate. Remember, a well-trained, reliable, and safe dog gets to enjoy a much bigger and more fulfilling and included life.

3) Training Approach: We believe humans should be in charge. We're unapologetic about this stance. We believe much of the problem behavior stems from this leadership vacuum. We subscribe to a less-is-more training approach. We don't do fancy. We use a short list of commands (sit, down, place, come, heel, crate, and no). We've built a training approach on real-life success. This means, the training has to deliver results, AND it has to be simple enough and practical enough for owners to incorporate into everyday life. Much of the training is passive, meaning the focus is on more stationary work than constant action work (tons of duration work). We also focus much more on calm and cool behavior than we do high-energy, constant motion, overly-alert dogs.

4) State of Mind/Comprehensive Focus: Rather than going after symptoms and chasing a never ending stream of issues, we go after the entire mindset of the dog. By sharing believable leadership, training tons of calmness, cultivating massive impulse control, sharing valuable consequences for poor choices, removing stress and anxiety by creating clarity and an overall lifestyle, we address the whole dog, not just the symptoms he's sharing. Once you teach a dog how to truly relax, turn off when asked, be respectful, and to defer to humans in a healthy fashion, you'll see most issues disappear.

5) Exercise, Play, and Affection: You can't just have all work all the time! It all needs to be kept in balance. But these should be things that your dog earns through great behavior—not just stuff he gets *just because.* The quickest way to send the wrong message to your dog, and make positive changes super difficult is to offer this soft, fun stuff before you've created respect. Typically when working to turn problem behaviors around, and creating more healthy relationships, we go super light on this stuff, if at all, and slowly add it in as the dog and relationship progress. You absolutely don't want to share soft, affectionate, playful stuff with a dog in an unhealthy or disrespectful space. But as things progress, you can start to strategically share more of this stuff. Let good behavior earn good stuff.

This is of course just an overview. But I hope it gives you some perspective on the big picture, and our approach and priorities.

We truly believe that if you can wrap your head around these 5 pieces of the puzzle, tweak and adjust, and do your best to actually put them into practice, you'd see massive changes in your dog and relationship.

it's just DOG TRAINING

One of the very best things to remind yourself while you're working through issues with your dog...

It's just dog training.

Keep it in its proper perspective. It's important, no doubt. We all want the best for our dogs and ourselves, but perspective is a magical thing. And remembering all the truly challenging, hard, painful things going on in the world can be just the ticket to help you relax, and put your dog training right where it belongs.

Important. But still,

just dog training.

Leading is something you do even when it's uncomfortable...

Leading is something you do even when you're tired...

Leading is something you do even if it creates friction...

Leading is something you do even when you've been away all day and are wracked with guilt...

Leading is prioritizing the needs of those in your care over your own comfort...

Leading is giving.
Leading is clarity.
Leading is selflessness.
Leading is kindness.
Leading is generous.
Leading is sharing wisdom.
Leading is sharing experience.
Leading is guiding.
Leading is helping.
Leading is loving.
Leading is showing the best way forward.
Leading is correcting when others are lost.
Leading is pulling the best out of others.
Leading is illuminating the path.
Leading is setting standards.
Leading is enforcing those standards.
Leading is creating an example through actions.
Leading is doing what's best over what's easiest.
Leading is knowing what's best and demanding it of others.
Leading is being okay with being unpopular.
Leading is understanding that tough love is still love.
Leading is short-term friction for long-term benefit.
Leading is finding your strength so you can help others find theirs.
Leading is safety.
Leading is dependable.
Leading is comfort.
Leading is love.

Leading is not something we do to someone; it's something we do for someone. It's not taking something from them; it's giving something to them.

It's the gift we give, and the responsibility we have, to those in our care, and those we care about.

Love them by leading them.

become a leader WORTH following

Okay, so by this point I'm pretty sure the whole "leadership thing being essential for a healthy relationship" is pretty clear.

We covered it from a multitude of angles. We've seen how its presence can bring out the very best in your dog, and its absence can bring out the worst.

Hopefully, if it all makes sense, you're feeling excited about the possibilities and inspired to work on cultivating your inner leader. But, you might also be feeling anxious, overwhelmed, and worried.

Where do I start? What if I don't have this leadership stuff? What if I want to make this a part of my new relationship dynamic with my dog...but I can't? What if I'm a big softie? What if I struggle with boundaries and permissiveness? What if DO lean too much on my dog, but can't seem to stop it?

These are all good questions. They're also super common. You're in good company. Most of us struggle in some capacity with this stuff. Most of us weren't taught to be leaders—and if we were, it was with humans. Our dogs have been our neutral zone. We kick butt at work but want to shed that pressure and responsibility once home.

A couple of things:

Leaders don't need to be perfect. In fact, I don't know any leader who would characterize themselves in that fashion. We're all flawed. There ain't no getting around that one. But the good news is, you don't have to be perfect to lead. You also don't need (and wouldn't be able even if you wanted) to become an awesome leader straight away.

This is all about the journey. (Yeah, that tired, but true, old saw.) No matter how committed and determined you are, you're not going to transform yourself overnight. You can transform your behavior and actions overnight, but who you are at the core? That's gonna take some time. And a lot of effort...if you want it.

This is where the whole dog training thing takes on that fascinating, and unexpected dimension. The opportunity dimension. The dimension where you get to focus on developing personal skills that you might be missing. Skills that might be creating problems in your relationship with your dog...and elsewhere. Skills that might, if no real consequence was at stake, not get prioritized.

Of course, this is all entirely optional. No one is going to force you to work on yourself. You can do as much or as little as you want. But know this: these issues you're seeing bubble up with you and your dog are bubbling up everywhere. Your dog just does an awesome job of illuminating and highlighting all the action.

All the things I listed as possible issues between you and your dog are issues we often see challenge our clients in their "regular" life as well.

Your boundary issues don't live in a vacuum. Your neediness doesn't exist only in dog land. Your self-worth issues will undermine the quality of your entire life. Your loneliness will follow you...everywhere.

And if these things are in play, and if we're not working on them, we're definitely not leading our dogs or ourselves.

Being a leader isn't a right, it's a privilege you earn. A privilege you earn through effort and daily focus.

Want to turn things around with your dog? Cool, make sure you're being honest and doing the same with yourself. Make sure you're doing your work to earn the right to lead.

Like I said, you don't have to be perfect to lead. Dogs and people don't require it. What we do require is effort, character, integrity, and resolve.

If you're working every day to be better than yesterday, you're leading. You're leading your way to a better life, and you're leading your way to being a person your dog can honor, follow, respect, and trust.

You're becoming a leader worth following.

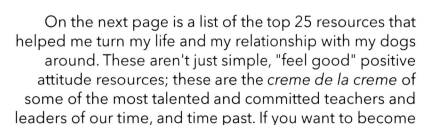

On the next page is a list of the top 25 resources that helped me turn my life and my relationship with my dogs around. These aren't just simple, "feel good" positive attitude resources; these are the *creme de la creme* of some of the most talented and committed teachers and leaders of our time, and time past. If you want to become someone worth following, I suggest you start here. Do the work, make the commitment, and as your skills and insights grow, so will the rest of your life...

RESOURCES

1) Art of Exceptional Living (6 Disc set)/ The Challenge To Succeed (2 Disc Set) - **Jim Rohn**
2) Compound Effect/Entrepreneur Rollercoaster - **Darren Hardy**
3) As a Man Thinketh - **James Allen**
4) The Success Principles - **Jack Canfield**
5) Psycho-Cybernetics - **Maxwell Maltz**
6) The Go-Giver - **Bob Burg**
7) See You at the Top - **Zig Ziglar**
8) The Slight Edge - **Jeff Olson**
9) The Power of Intention - **Wayne Dyer**
10) Shut Up, Stop Whining, and Get a Life/You're Broke Because You Want To Be/It's called Work For A Reason/Your Kids Are Your Own Fault/Grow A Pair - **Larry Winget**
11) Crush It/Thank You Economy/#AskGaryVee - **Gary Vaynerchuk**
12) The Little Gold Book Of Yes Attitude - **Jeffrey Gitomer**
13) Goals: 2 CD set - **Zig Ziglar**
14) Be Obsessed Or Be Average - **Grant Cardone**
15) How To Win Friends And Influence People - **Dale Carnegie**
16) Think And Grow Rich - **Napoleon Hill**
17) The War of Art/Do The Work/Turning Pro - **Steven Pressfield**
18) Why You're Dumb, Sick And Broke - **Randy Gage**
19) The Magic Of Thinking Big - **David Schwartz**
20) Rich Dad Poor Dad - **Robert Kiyosaki**
21) The Gifts of Imperfection/Daring Greatly/Rising Strong - **Brene Brown**
22) 4 Hour Work Week/Tools Of Titans - **Tim Ferriss**
23) The Richest Man In Babylon - **George Clason**
24) The Icarus Deception/Tribes/What To Do When It's Your Turn - **Seth Godin**
25) The Obstacle Is The Way/Ego Is The Enemy - **Ryan Holiday**

Seth Godin's Blog
Randy Gage's Blog
Darren Hardy's "Darren Daily" (email mentoring)
Bob Burg's Blog
Gary Vaynerchuck's Facebook/Instagram/YouTube
Casey Neistat's YouTube Channel
The Rock's Instagram
Tim Ferriss' podcast

afterward

We made it! Thanks for taking the time to actually read this far! (Do you know the stats on how many people don't finish books? You don't want to know!)

I'll be honest, being my first book, and of course wanting it to be awesome, it's been quite the journey. Trying to find the right mix of information, and presenting it in a fashion that connects and makes sense, has been an incredible challenge. And a huge responsibility. And one I take very seriously. Being such a dog loving world, and yet seeing so many owners and dogs struggle and suffer due to a lack of information, has been a mission I've felt compelled to try to help move forward.

Seeing the gaps in understanding, seeing the mistakes made repeatedly (with good intentions), and seeing so much unnecessary struggle...well, it's enough to get you fired up to try to write a book!

Another aspect of the mission has been to give dog owners another voice or option to check out. With all the incredibly noisy dog training propaganda out there, it's close to impossible to make sense of it all. I wanted to make sure there was a voice for the other side of things. I wanted to share real-world experience, rather than ideology or agenda. Everything in this book is based on what I've personally seen work, and not work. There's nothing in here based on cherry-picked studies, or supposedly "modern, updated, science-backed" ideology. I have no desire to brainwash you or bring you over to the "dark side". My only goal is to share, honestly, and what I've shared here is simply what I've seen after many, many dogs.

They are, after all, the real experts.

With so much information out there that directly contradicts the other, I can't imagine being an owner with a dog who has issues, and trying to make sense of it all. My heart goes out to anyone trying to figure this stuff out. Truly.

My deepest hope is that at least a few of the ideas and concepts presented here will open up some mental doors. I hope they'll make some new connections and turn on some light bulbs.

The goal with LTBLT was to present our dogs, and the issues we often create and/or encounter, through a different lens. A lens of simplicity and common sense. A lens that views many of the issues your dog might be dealing with, through the same, or similar view as your own. When we can see things as they do, it can make a huge difference in our ability to understand and help.

My sincere hope is that this book allows you to understand things between you and your dog a little more clearly. A little deeper. But also, without all the training jargon that makes so much of this stuff so challenging for most owners to make sense of. I purposely left it non-scienc-y. Not dumbed down, but more tangible and clear. Hopefully, if I did my job right, you'll walk away from this book seeing and understanding your dog and yourself, more clearly.

When all is said and done, I hope I've managed to reconnect readers to some simple truths. Truths that we've either lost, or become uncomfortable with. Truths about the gift of leadership. Truths about how structure, guidance, rules, expectations, accountability, and experience...when shared, with the goal of helping and creating clarity and comfort...are nothing like the unfortunate modern interpretations of what leadership means. And that whether it's your dog, your child, a friend, or an employee, showing the way for others to follow, with the intent to help them improve and find their best, is the furthest thing from a negative. It's actually the greatest, most un-selfish act you can share with another.

Leadership to me is: "Here, let me help. I know the way."

thank you

Okay!! So this is actually the best part of the book...for me! Two reasons. One, it means we've actually wrapped this baby!! And two, it means I get a chance to thank all the wonderful people in my life who've helped make this dream a reality.

First, I want to thank Junior, Oakley, and Belle. Without the three original scoundrels, and all they taught me, I wouldn't be doing what I'm doing, and this book certainly wouldn't exist. You three were my family, my friends, my daily exercise and adventure companions, and you made a life that was dark and lonely, bright and hopeful and filled with love. Thank you from the bottom of my heart.

To Carolyn Bender, my very first client, for taking a chance on me, befriending me, cheering me on, and for seeing my potential. To all my mentors, both virtual and real, thank you for always pushing me to reach for my best. To my family for always cheering on my dog adventures and never trying to squeeze me into a conventional life...and for putting up with me. It's a blessing to have a family that encourages you to follow whatever your passions are, without judgement.

To the TGD crew, Laura, Brittany, Shelby, Anri, Tony, Cambre, and Alexis...thank you for always teaching. I've learned so much from all of you. Thanks for pushing me to be my best and thanks for giving your best. None of this would work without you and all the amazingness that each of you bring! Thanks to Jeff Gellman and his awesome family for treating me like one of their own. Jeff, what an adventure it's all been buddy! Thanks to all the T3 students who have pushed me to be a better teacher and leader. I love all of you. Thanks to all of the amazing clients who have trusted us with their dogs. We wouldn't be here without you guys. Your belief and trust is why we exist. To all the fans and supporters who follow us on social media, thank you for being part of our extended family. I appreciate you guys and all your love, support, and kindness sooooo much! And lastly, thank you to my amazing business partner and great friend, Laura Morgan. The great team, the culture we have, the DVDs, T3, the success of TGD, this book, and so much more, wouldn't exist without your constant encouragement, belief, and amazing yin to my yang. Thanks so much for filling the gaps and making this dream a reality.

And of course, thank you for buying the book. By doing so, you support the bigger mission: finding our way towards truly understanding our dogs and ourselves. And that through that understanding we can all have the chance to live more happy, balanced, and fulfilled lives.

Made in the USA
Columbia, SC
12 March 2023